Developed by Contemporary Books, Inc., and General Learning Corporation, Northbrook, Illinois

Published by Contemporary Books, Inc.
180 North Michigan Avenue
Chicago, Illinois 60601
Manufactured in the United States of America
International Standard Book Number: 0-8092-4018-1

Published simultaneously in Canada by
Fitzhenry & Whiteside
91 Granton Drive
Richmond Hill, Ontario L4B 2N5
Canada

Library of Congress Cataloging-in-Publication Data

Amazing century.
p. cm.
Includes indexes.
Contents: bk. 1. 1900–1929 – bk. 2. 1929–1945 – bk. 3. 1945–1960
ISBN 0-8092-4020-3 (pbk. : v. 1). – ISBN 0-8092-4018-1 (pbk. : v. 2). – ISBN 0-8092-4017-3 (pbk. : v. 3)
1. United States – Civilization – 20th century. 2. Civilization, Modern – 20th century. I. Contemporary Books, inc.
E169.1.A47186 1992 91-35292
973.9 – dc20 CIP

Editorial Director
Caren Van Slyke

Assistant Editorial Director
Mark Boone

Project Editor
Pat Fiene

Editorial
Chris Benton
Sarah Conroy

Editorial Production Manager
Norma Fioretti

Cover Design
Georgene Sainati

Cover Photo
Library of Congress

Executive Editor
Laura Ruekberg

Managing Editor
Alan Lenhoff

Associate Editor
Miriam Greenblatt

Art Director
Ami Koenig

Research
David Bristow
Sam Johnson
Terese Noto
Therese Shinners
Betty Tsamis
Deborah Weise

To Our Readers

The hunger and hurt of the Great Depression . . . the fierce battles of World War II . . . the race to make the first atomic bomb . . . the skill and grace of Jesse Owens, Joe Louis, and Babe Didrikson . . .

In the pages of this book are some of the biggest new stories of their day – stories that touched the hearts and minds of our grandparents and great-grandparents. The photographs and stories in this book reach out to us. They tell about people and events that have helped to shape this century – and make our nation what it is today.

Though you may not know all the faces and places, you'll recognize many of the stories behind them. You'll see that today's news stories have their roots in the past – and that we have many things in common with the people who came before us. We learn from their tragedies and benefit from their triumphs.

In pictures and in words, each of the books in the *Amazing Century* series highlights a different time period in this century. See for yourself. Thumb through the pages of this and all the *Amazing Century* books, and discover the way we were.

The Editors

America and the World

Lifestyles

Arts and Entertainment

Contents

Sports

Money Matters

Crime, Punishment, and the Law

Science and Technology

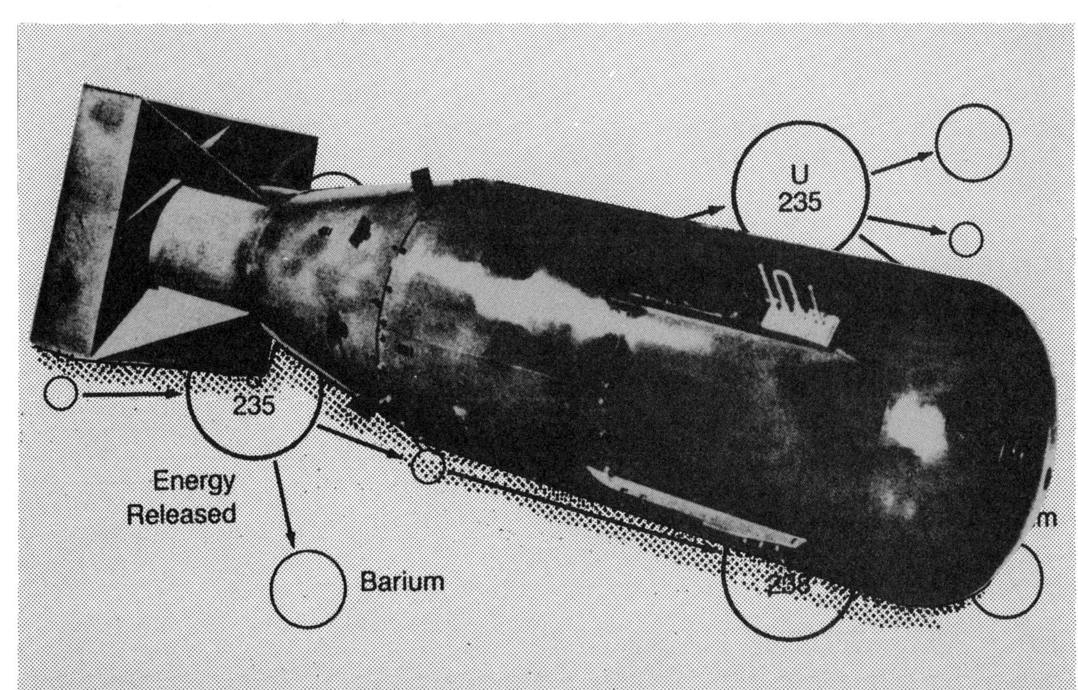

TIMELINE

1929
U.S. stock market crashes; Great Depression begins

1931
Japan invades Manchuria, triggering war in East Asia

1933
20th Amendment states that Congress must meet at least once a year and sets January 20 as end date of presidential terms

21st Amendment ends Prohibition, the "no alcohol" law

Federal Reserve Act of 1933 rebuilds U.S. banking system

1935
Italy invades Ethiopia

1936
Jesse Owens wins four gold medals in Berlin Summer Olympics

1937
Boxer Joe Louis begins 12-year reign as heavyweight champion

San Francisco's Golden Gate Bridge sets new record as world's longest

Pilot Amelia Earhart and navigator Fred Noonan disappear over Pacific Ocean during around-the-world flight

31st–32d U.S. Presidents

Herbert Hoover (1929–1932)	Franklin Roosevelt (1933–1937)

1929	1930	1931	1932	1933	1934	1935	1936	1937

1939

Germany and Italy align in Pact of Steel

Germany invades Poland; Great Britain and France declare war

Soviet Union invades Baltic countries

1940

Germany invades Low Countries, Denmark, Norway, and France; begins attacks on Great Britain

Germany, Italy, Japan align in Tripartite Pact

1941

Germany invades Soviet Union

Japan attacks U.S. military bases in Hawaii and Philippines; United States declares war

1942

U.S. Manhattan Project begins development of atomic bomb

Allies win Battle of El Alamein, a turning point of war in Africa

Allies win Battle of Midway, a turning point of war in Pacific

1943

Germany retreats from Soviet Union

Allies invade Sicily; Italy surrenders

1944

Allies' invasion of Normandy frees France, a turning point of war in Europe

1945

Germany surrenders to Allies

United States drops atomic bombs on Hiroshima and Nagasaki, Japan

Japan surrenders to Allies

Franklin Roosevelt							Harry Truman
1938	1939	1940	1941	1942	1943	1944	1945

Hard Times

Nineteen twenty-nine started out as a very good year. President Herbert Hoover announced, "We in America today are nearer to the final triumph over poverty than ever before in the history of any land. The poorhouse is vanishing from us."

But Hoover spoke too soon. In October of 1929, the stock market crashed. By mid-November, the value of stocks, or shares in the nation's business, had dropped more than $30 billion. This was almost as much money as the United States had spent on World War I. And the worst was yet to come.

Huge losses in the stock market resulted in huge losses in business. People stopped buying things they did not absolutely need. As sales fell, worried business owners began to look for ways to cut costs. They held back on their plans to expand their business, cut back on production and buying, and laid off employees. The Great Depression – the worst economic downturn in the nation's history – had taken root.

From Bad to Worse

Over the next three years, people kept hoping that the economy would improve. It didn't get better, however. By 1932, about 85,000 businesses had closed their doors, and nearly 13 million workers – one in every four – were unemployed. Thousands of families lost their homes because they could not afford to make the payments on their loans. Farmers also had trouble paying off their mortgages, and about 400,000 lost their homes as well as their land. About 6,000 banks – one in every four – failed, wiping out the savings of 9 million of their customers.

Hungry people stood in line for free meals at soup kitchens run by religious and charitable organizations. Some picked through garbage cans, searching for scraps of food. On the edges of cities, homeless people lived in "Hoovervilles" – camps made up of

shacks, homemade tents, rusting cars, and cardboard boxes.

In some areas, schools closed because there was no money to pay teachers. Some cities did not even have enough money to pay for police officers and fire fighters.

Who's in Charge?

The American people were becoming angry. They pointed the finger of blame at Herbert Hoover and his administration. As the anger grew, so did the danger of violence. Some people even feared that the government might be overthrown. The head of a farmers' organization warned, "Unless something is done for the American farmer, we will have a revolution in the countryside in 12 months." Riots by people demanding food broke out in many cities. The anger was also directed at business owners and bankers.

President Hoover did take a few steps toward helping the American

A "Hooverville" in Seattle, Washington, 1933.

On the day that Roosevelt becomes president, he talks with outgoing President Hoover.

Hoover: Symbol of Poverty

President Hoover's name came to stand for poverty and misery during the Depression years. In a bitter joke on the president, people began calling homeless families' makeshift camps "Hoovervilles." This word gave rise to several other terms:

- Hoover Hiltons – Hoovervilles near wealthy neighborhoods;
- Hoover blankets – old newspapers stuffed under clothing for warmth;
- Hoover flags – empty pants pockets turned inside out;
- Hoover wagons – trucks pulled by mules;
- Hoover ham – dead animals left at the side of the road.

economy. For example, he set up an agency to lend money to businesses and another agency to help farmers and homeowners pay their mortgages. In general, though, Hoover did not think the government should do much about the Depression. The United States had had depressions before, and they had always ended after a few years. He was sorry if people were hungry or homeless – he was not a heartless man – but he did not believe that the federal government should help individuals. He felt that they should rely on private charities for help. Handouts from the federal government, Hoover believed, would weaken people's self-respect. "This is not an issue as to whether people will go cold and hungry in the United States," he said. "It is solely a question of the best method by which hunger and cold shall be prevented."

In 1932, the Republican party again ran Hoover for president. The Democratic party nominated Franklin Delano Roosevelt, often called by his initials, FDR. Roosevelt, unlike Hoover, believed the federal government should take strong measures to end the Depression. FDR believed the federal government should take responsibility for people's economic well-being. "The duty of the state toward the citizens," he said, "is the duty of the servant to his master." The American people agreed – and elected FDR by a wide margin. ■

How do you think a depression affects the way people feel about money? Are people who have lived through a depression likely to feel more hopeful or less hopeful about the future?

Nothing to Fear but Fear

"I pledge you, I pledge myself, to a new deal for the American people."
–Franklin Delano Roosevelt, July 1932

Americans had been angry enough to vote out the old president. But what did they know about the new one? Franklin Delano Roosevelt had been governor of New York State and assistant secretary of the navy. He had also run for vice president. Clearly, he was experienced in politics and government. But he was a rich man who had grown up with all the comforts that money could buy. Could he understand the problems of the poor? Would he care about the hungry and the homeless?

FDR's legs were almost paralyzed from polio, and he could barely walk, even on crutches. Would he have the strength and energy to run the country during such troubled times?

The answer to all these questions was yes. FDR was a strong leader. For one thing, he really loved people and cared about the poor. He also realized that what Americans needed more than anything else was confidence. They needed to feel hopeful about the future. They needed to feel that someone strong and trustworthy was in charge. They needed to be told that no matter how many troubles the nation faced, solutions could–and would–be found. FDR set the tone for his presidency when he said, "The only thing we have to fear is fear itself." People took comfort from this hopeful attitude.

FDR was also a practical person. He believed that "It is common sense to take a method and try it. If it fails, admit it frankly and try another." Many people felt that FDR's active, commonsense approach to government was a refreshing change.

On the Air

FDR was the first president to use radio to explain his ideas to the American people. He had a warm, reassuring voice, and he spoke clearly and simply. He talked to people–whom he called "my friends and fellow Americans"–as if he were having a private conversation with them in their living room. For this reason, FDR's radio speeches came to be known as "fireside chats." People loved them. After the first fireside chat, for example, Americans sent the president 500,000 letters in just one week. ■

FDR talks to the nation in a radio "fireside chat."

New Deal, New Programs

The WPA gave work to many people, including artists.

One of FDR's first goals as president was to put people back to work. He saw nothing wrong with the government's creating jobs for people so that they could earn money and regain their self-respect.

One such jobs program was the Civilian Conservation Corps, or CCC. It was aimed at young men from 18 to 25 years old. They were put to work building roads, cleaning up beaches, and, especially, planting trees. Between 1933 and 1941, they planted more than 200 million trees on the Great Plains, from Canada all the way to Mexico. The "green belt" they created helped keep the soil on the Great Plains from being blown away by the wind.

Another jobs program was the Works Progress Administration, or WPA. WPA workers built about 600 airports around the country and built or improved more than 100,000 hospitals, libraries, and schools. The WPA also supported the arts. It gave work to hundreds of artists, writers, musicians, and actors. WPA musicians gave free public concerts. WPA actors put on plays in 16 foreign languages as well as English. Your local post office may have a mural, or wall painting, that was painted by a WPA artist.

A different kind of program was the Tennessee Valley Authority, or TVA. The Tennessee Valley was one of the poorest parts of the country. Over the years, people had cut down the original forests. As a result, floods washed away the soil, and farmers found it hard to grow crops. In addition, many of the homes and farms in the valley lacked electricity. Under the TVA, a series of dams was built across the Tennessee River and its branches. The dams supplied cheap electric power and helped prevent floods. The dams also created lakes where people could go boating, fishing, and swimming.

Americans referred to these new agencies as "alphabet soup," because they were better known by their initials than their full names. In all, 18 government agencies were set up under the New Deal. Among other things, they regulated the stock market to prevent another crash, set up minimum wages for certain types of work, and provided benefits for elderly people.

A Good Deal?

By the early 1940s, the New Deal was over. Did it succeed?

If you look just at the economy, the answer is both yes and no. Unemployment was cut in half. Banks were no longer failing, some farmers and factory workers were earning more money, the Hoovervilles were deserted, and most people had enough to eat. On the other hand, about 8 million Americans still lacked jobs. And the New Deal jobs programs cost a lot of money. The federal government was deeply in debt.

In other ways, though, the New Deal was a success. Many Americans regained their confidence, both in themselves and in their system of government. People in other nations turned to dictators to try to solve their problems. People in the United States continued to believe in democracy. ■

Roosevelt's New Deal was a change in the relationship between the government and the American people. What do you think that relationship should be? Should the government be responsible for making sure that people have medical care? Food? Do you think you would have supported the New Deal if you had been an American citizen in the 1930s?

Some politicians today think the government should set up a CCC to work in our big cities. What projects might such an agency do?

CCC workers (above) pulling up two-year-old fir trees for transplanting. WPA workers (below) at their sewing machines in 1937.

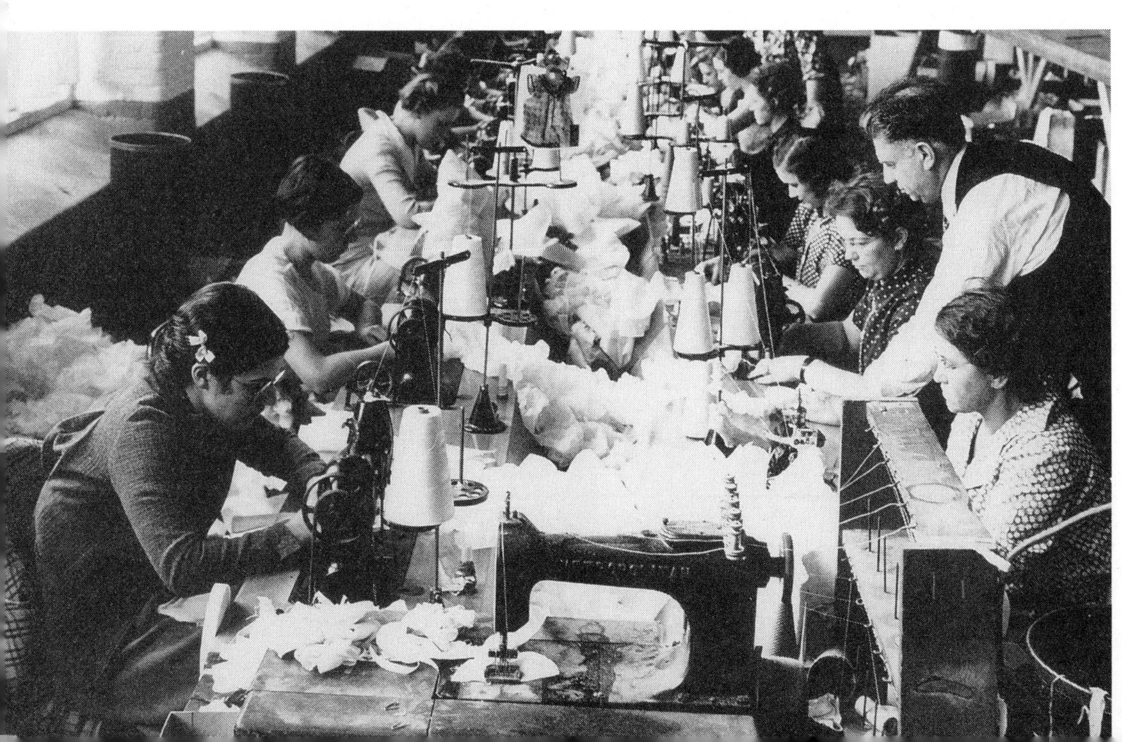

Storm Clouds of War

After World War I ended in 1918, many Americans had lost interest in foreign affairs. They did not want to get involved in other countries' problems. They had lost family and friends in the war and were angry because the Allies could not repay the billions of dollars the United States had lent them. Most Americans felt that the United States should mind its own business.

By 1939, however, many Americans were once again paying attention to events overseas. They were troubling events that gradually involved the United States.

Trouble in Asia

The Great Depression affected not just the United States but nations all over the world. Among those that were hit hardest was Japan.

Japan is a small country with few natural resources such as oil, iron for steel, and land. As a result, it must sell manufactured goods to other nations so it can buy food and raw materials. But the Great Depression caused world trade to collapse. This left Japan unable to feed its people.

For a number of years, Japanese generals and admirals had been urging the country to solve its problems by taking control of part of Asia. As the Depression continued, the Japanese government decided to take the advice of its military. By 1932, Japan had taken control of the Chinese province of Manchuria, with its vast supplies of coal and iron ore. Five years later, in 1937, Japanese troops took over most of China's coastal area, including its major cities. Millions of Chinese moved inland, and China and Japan were at war.

Many experts in world affairs warned that Japan would not stop with China. They believed Japan would attack British, Dutch, and French colonies in the Pacific to get their oil, tin, and rubber. A few experts even believed that Japan would attack the Philippine Islands, which belonged to the United States.

Trouble in Europe

The situation in Europe was even more frightening than the situation in Asia. The reason was a German dictator named Adolf Hitler.

Like the United States and Japan,

HITLER MADE CHANCELLOR OF GERMANY
BUT COALITION CABINET LIMITS POWER;
CENTRISTS HOLD BALANCE IN REICHSTA

Pledges Fight in Cabin

Germany was hit hard by the Great Depression. By 1932, two out of five German workers were unemployed. In addition, the country was still hurting from its defeat in World War I. It wanted revenge.

Hitler became Germany's ruler just five weeks before FDR began his first term as president. But the two men acted very differently in office. FDR tackled his country's problems within a democratic framework. Hitler destroyed German democracy and prepared his country for war.

Under Hitler, only the Nazi party was allowed to exist. Other political parties were banned. The government controlled all the mass media. It burned books that contained ideas it didn't like. Secret police spied on people everywhere. Churches were controlled, and labor unions were banned. Anyone who objected to what Hitler was doing was sent to a concentration camp, a type of prison. Most political prisoners were never seen again.

At the same time, Hitler began arming Germany. By 1936, the government was spending three-fourths of its budget on tanks, guns, and other weapons. Hitler was determined to create a new German empire, the Third Reich. He said it would last for a thousand years.

In 1938, Hitler sent his troops into Austria, took over the government, and made Austria part of Germany. His excuse was that the 7 million Austrians, who spoke German, were really part of the German people. Next, he turned his attention to

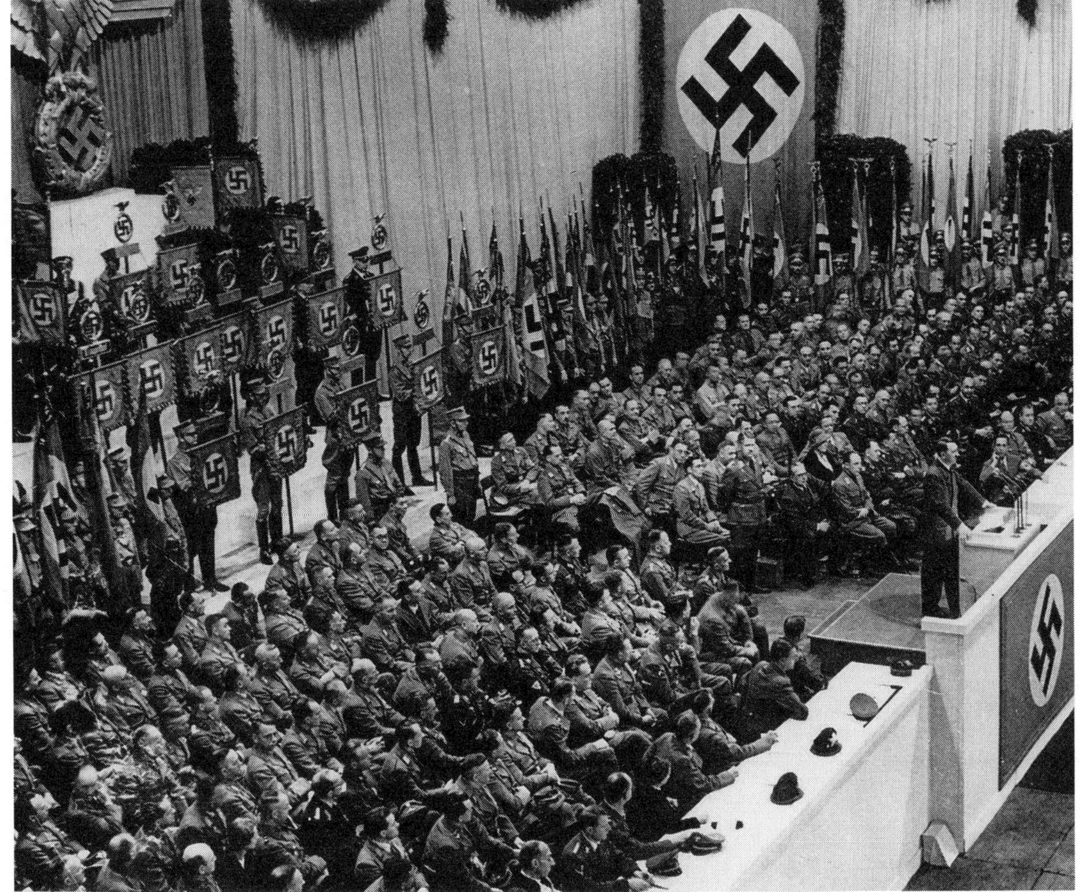

Hitler addressing the German people at a rally in 1941.

British prime minister Neville Chamberlain (left), shakes hands with Adolf Hitler after the two signed a peace agreement in 1938.

The map shows Europe before Hitler came to power.

Czechoslovakia, which contained about 3 million Germans. Hitler accused the Czech government of mistreating them and threatened to take action against the country.

At this point, Great Britain and France stepped in. They had suffered greatly during World War I, and they desperately wanted to avoid another war. Italy also stepped in. It was already involved in conflicts with other nations and was eager to avoid becoming involved in a war with Germany. British prime minister Neville Chamberlain, French premier Edouard Daladier, and Italian premier Benito Mussolini met with Hitler in Munich, Germany, in 1938. Hitler could have part of Czechoslovakia, they said, if he promised not to make any more demands for land. Hitler agreed, and the Munich Pact was signed in September of 1938.

When Chamberlain returned to Great Britain, he was a hero. "I believe it is peace for our time," he said. London newspapers compared him to Jesus and Abraham Lincoln.

But appeasement – giving in to Hitler – did not work. Within six months, Hitler broke his promise. On March 16, 1939, Hitler entered Prague, the capital of Czechoslovakia. German soldiers soon occupied the rest of the country. A week later, they took over part of Lithuania. And on September 1, 1939, they crossed the border of Poland. Within two days, most of Europe was at war. ■

When Iraq invaded Kuwait in 1990, many people compared the invasion to Germany's invading Czechoslovakia and Poland. They compared Saddam Hussein to Adolf Hitler.

Do you think the comparisons are fair? Why or why not? Do you approve of the actions the United States took against Iraq? Why or why not?

World War II

DAILY NEWS

THREE CENTS

Telephone DEArborn 1111.

65TH YEAR—141.

FRIDAY, JUNE 14, 1940—FORTY-FOUR PAGES.

PARIS FALLS!

'France Doomed, Britain Next'—Nazis

AMERICAS SAFE? ROOSEVELT CITES HITLER'S RECORD

'Total Collapse' Of Defense Seen

B. E. F. LEAVES AGAIN FOR WAR FRONT

English Prepare To Fight Alone

THREE CENTS

FRIDAY, SEPTEMBER 1, 1939—THIRTY-SIX PAGES.

NAZIS BOMB WARSAW; POLES DOWN 16 PLANES

Hitler Challenge Hurled to World

Fuehrer in Deadly Passion Vows to Conquer Poland or Die as Reichstag Cheers His Order to Battle.

BULLETIN.

STOP FIGHTING OR WE'LL ACT: CHAMBERLAIN

Commons Cheers Premier's Declaration; Votes

NOTICE

In view of the War situation The Daily News will publish all editions Monday, Labor Day.

Latest War

ITALY DECIDES TO BE NEUTRAL FOR TIME BEING

No Action Planned as Long as Only Germany and Poles Are Involved.

Word Picture Of Air Raid

Scene as German Warplanes Swooped on Polish Capital Is Vividly Described by Eyewitness.

World War II began in September of 1939, when Great Britain and France came to Poland's aid. But in less than a month, German armies had conquered Poland. They employed a new tactic known as *blitzkrieg*, or lightning war. First, waves of dive-bombers blasted Polish planes on the ground. Then they destroyed railroads and supply depots. At the same time, masses of tanks smashed through Polish defenses. The tanks were followed by soldiers, many of them on motorcycles or in armored trucks. They were soon joined by troops from Germany's ally, the Soviet Union, which invaded Poland from the east. The Soviet Union also invaded Estonia, Latvia, Lithuania, and Finland.

A map of Europe (above) just before the Nazis invaded Poland. Smoke rising from London (below) during Nazi bombing.

The following spring, Hitler struck again. Within three months, his blitzkrieg overwhelmed Denmark, Norway, the Netherlands, Belgium, Luxembourg, and France. Great Britain was left standing almost alone.

The British, however, refused to give up. As their new prime minister, Winston Churchill, said: ". . .We shall defend our island, whatever the cost may be, we shall fight on the beaches, we shall fight on the landing grounds, we shall fight in the fields and in the streets, we shall fight in the hills, we shall never surrender."

In August of 1940, Hitler launched an all-out air attack on Great Britain. He hoped to destroy British morale before invading the country. Night after night, German bombers pounded London and other cities. But the British held firm. For three months, pilots of the Royal Air Force rose to battle their enemies in the sky. On the ground, civilians calmly put out fires, cleared away the bomb damage, and cared for the wounded. By October 31, Hitler was forced to give up his dream of invasion. The Battle of Britain was over.

Hitler then turned his attention eastward. First, he swept through the Balkans, in southeastern Europe. Then, in June of 1941, he launched a blitzkrieg against his former ally, the Soviet Union.

As Europe burned, America watched. Most Americans did not want to get involved in a conflict thousands of miles away. But in Washington, President Roosevelt persuaded Congress to start the country's first peacetime draft. He believed the country should be prepared to defend itself. ■

America at War

"Yesterday, December 7, 1941—a date which will live in infamy—the United States of America was suddenly and deliberately attacked by naval and air forces of the Empire of Japan."
—Franklin Delano Roosevelt,
War Message to Congress

Japan's sneak attack on the U.S. naval base at Pearl Harbor, Hawaii, killed 2,402 Americans and wounded another 1,178. The Japanese destroyed or damaged 19 ships and over 100 planes. At the same time, the Japanese attacked the Philippines, where they destroyed almost every American plane. These were damaging blows. But Americans responded with determination. They had one goal: victory. The American people were united by Pearl Harbor.

Pearl Harbor under attack on December 7, 1941—a day that *has* "lived in infamy."

The Home Front

For some time, the United States had been sending weapons to Great Britain, the Soviet Union, and China. Now, as federal money poured out for defense contracts, American factories organized for total war production. Soon, tens of thousands of planes, tanks, guns, and ships were rolling off the assembly lines. As a result, unemployment disappeared.

Everyone pitched in to help the war effort. People formed car pools so they could ride together and save gasoline. They collected scrap metal, rubber, and other materials to recycle. Also, as their bank accounts grew, they bought war bonds, a way of lending the government money to help pay for the war. After the war ended, the government paid back the loans with interest.

Another way civilians became part of the war effort was through the rationing of goods needed by the armed forces. Rationing meant limiting the amount of goods that people could buy. The government gave out books of ration stamps. Civilians had to use the stamps as well as money whenever they bought such items as meat, shoes, coffee, sugar, butter, canned food, and cotton and woolen clothing. If they ran out of stamps, they could not buy any more rationed goods.

Every evening after dinner, people switched on their radios to hear the latest news from overseas. The living rooms of America rang with the names of unfamiliar places like Java, Rangoon, and Bataan. When American and English troops invaded Africa, their families back home heard about it on the evening news.

D-Day: June 6, 1944. The Allies landing in Normandy, France. The invasion was the turning point of the war against Germany.

The map shows the movement of Allied troops, 1939–1945.

Defeating Germany

The United States faced a two-front war against Germany and Japan. Which enemy should it try to defeat first?

Roosevelt and Churchill decided to concentrate on Germany. In November of 1942, they succeeded in defeating Nazi troops at the Battle of El Alamein, in North Africa. That winter, the Soviet Union scored a major victory at the Battle of Stalingrad. The German armed forces began to retreat.

On June 6, 1944, American, British, and other Allied forces crossed the English Channel and landed on the beaches of Normandy, in France. It was the largest land and sea operation in history. And despite heavy losses, it was a success. By the end of August, Paris was free. In late April 1945, Hitler committed suicide, and Germany surrendered on May 7. Roosevelt, however, did not live to see the Allied victory. He had died of a stroke less than a month earlier.

THEN & NOW

After World War II, Germany's borders were changed, and the country was divided into two parts. East Germany became a Communist nation allied with the Soviet Union. West Germany had a capitalist economy and was allied with the United States, among other nations. Because living conditions were so much better in West Germany, thousands of East Germans kept leaving for the West. In 1961, a wall was built across Berlin to cut off the stream of refugees. Finally, in 1989, the Berlin Wall came down. The next year, the two Germanys again became one nation. Germans rejoiced: the war was finally over.

Source: U.S. Department of Defense

The arrows show the Allied strategy of "island hopping" in the Pacific during World War II.

Defeating Japan

At first, the war against Japan went badly. The Japanese conquered the Philippines and most of Southeast Asia. By the spring of 1942, their armies threatened India and Australia. Then came the Battle of Midway, in which an American fleet destroyed a Japanese fleet that was headed for Hawaii. Amazingly, the two fleets never saw each other. All the fighting was done by carrier-based airplanes.

From 1943 on, American forces in the Pacific used a strategy called "island hopping." They attacked major Japanese island bases but bypassed smaller ones. By October of 1944, American troops were back in the Philippines. Soon after, they landed on the islands of Iwo Jima and Okinawa. Now they were within bombing range of Japan's major cities.

On the morning of August 6, 1945, American planes dropped the world's first atomic bomb on the city of Hiroshima, Japan. President Harry S. Truman announced, "The force from which the sun draws its power has been loosed against those who brought war to the Far East." Three days later, a second atomic bomb was dropped, this time on the city of Nagasaki. On August 14, the emperor of Japan ordered his people to surrender.

Americans celebrated the end of the war with great outdoor rallies and parades. Six years after Hitler's armies marched into Poland, World War II was finally over. But the cost was tremendous. About 56 million people – both soldiers and civilians – had died. And much of the world lay in ruins. ■

There are still many Americans alive who remember the bombing of Pearl Harbor and the invasion of Normandy. Interview an older American who lived through World War II about his or her memories of wartime. Write up the interview in a "question and answer" format.

Philosopher George Santayana once wrote, "Those who cannot remember the past are condemned to repeat it." What do you think we can learn from studying World War II? How can we learn enough to avoid repeating mistakes?

Hiroshima lies in ruins from a single bomb. A U.S. newspaper announces the end of the war.

TUESDAY, AUGUST 14, 1945–TWENTY-SIX PAGES.

FOUR CENTS

WAR ENDS

Truman Announces Japanese Surrend

Child Reveals

A Crime Without a Name

You are six years old. One night, you wake up to find a gun in your face. A German soldier orders you to get out of bed and go outside with your family. He tells you to raise your hands above your head. The night air is cold. You are frightened as you are forced to climb into a large train car that usually holds cattle. As the train pulls away from the station, you fear you will never see your home again.

Days later, the train stops. You are hungry, thirsty, and very tired. Men in uniform roughly pull you off the train and force you to strip. You, your family, and many of your neighbors stand naked in a long line. A doctor moves along the line, inspecting each person. The strongest people go to a huge building where they will work. All the others go to a giant gas chamber where they will be suffocated by poison gas.

This happened to millions of Europeans during World War II. In addition to hating democracy and glorifying war, Adolf Hitler was a racist. He believed that the Germans were a "master race" that was destined

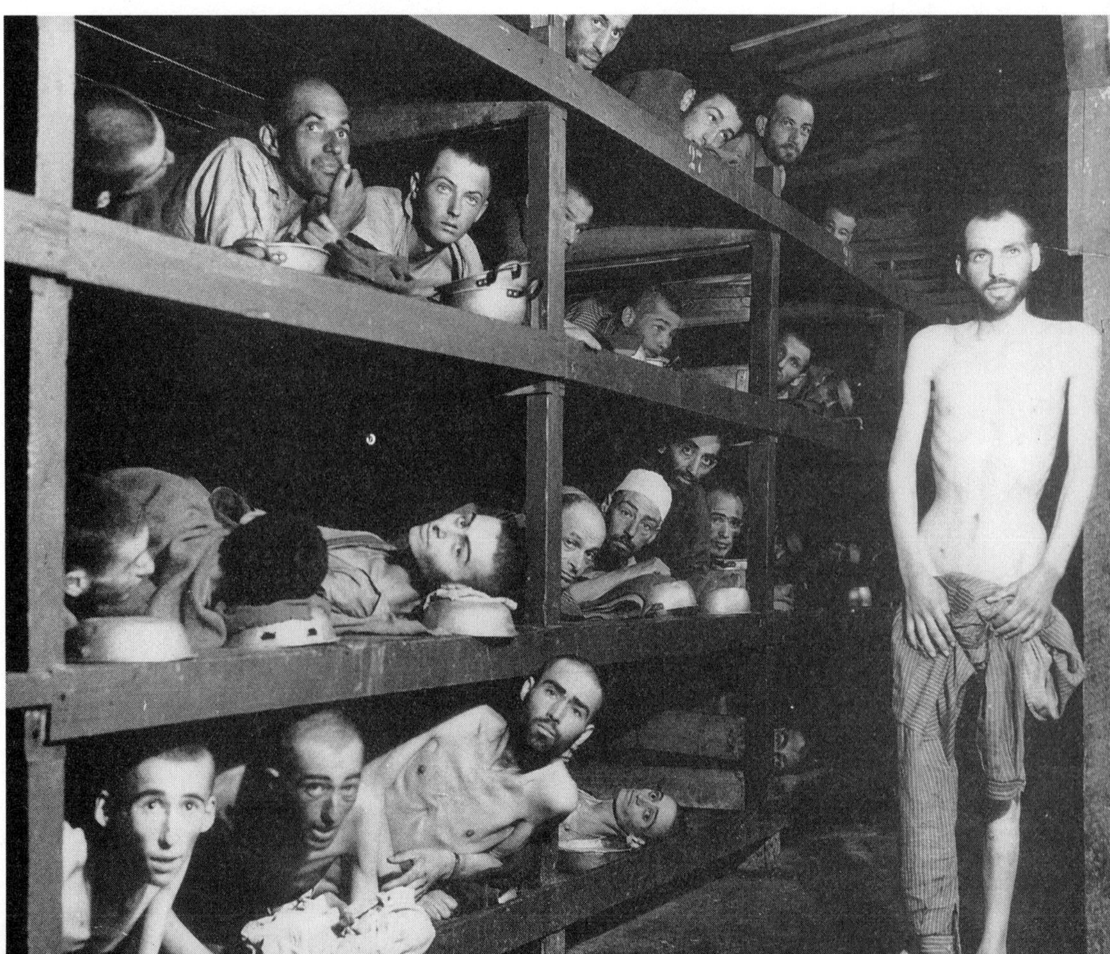

Concentration camp prisoners at Buchenwald.

to rule the world. Jews, Poles, Russians, and most nonwhites were "inferior races." They were fit only to be slaves for the Germans or to be killed.

The Jews were the main target of Hitler's campaign of hatred. Hitler had never accepted Germany's defeat in World War I. He refused to believe that German armies had been beaten. Instead, he blamed the Jews, saying they had "stabbed Germany in the back."

When Hitler came to power, he began a campaign against the Jews. First, he attacked them on the economic front. Jews were fired from government jobs. They were not allowed to practice law or medicine, to teach, or to farm. Then Hitler attacked the Jews on the political front. He took away their citizenship rights. They had to wear a yellow six-pointed star on their clothing so they could be identified easily.

In 1942, Hitler began to put into effect his plan to kill all Jews in Europe. He called it the "Final Solution." German soldiers in Poland and the Soviet Union shot almost 700,000 Jews. Then, death camps such as Auschwitz, Belzec, Chelmno, Maidanek, Sobibor, and Treblinka were set up to finish the job. In all, the Nazis murdered about 6 million Jews. Almost one-third were children under age six. This crime is known as the Holocaust. The Nazis also killed gypsies, homosexuals, and the mentally ill. In addition, about 6 million Russians and Poles were worked to death as slave laborers.

Winston Churchill called Hitler's actions "a crime without a name." He meant that Hitler's actions were so horrible that there are no words to describe them. After the war, about 500,000 Nazis were convicted of war crimes and received sentences. ■

A map of the concentration camps. In black boxes are names of camps used only for the murder of Jews. At Auschwitz alone, more than 2 million innocent people were murdered.

The Holocaust was one of the most horrible events of the 20th century. It raises many questions that don't have easy answers. Here are some to think about:

How could it have happened—especially in an educated, civilized nation such as Germany? Why was Hitler able to kill 6 million people for the crime of existing? Why didn't the German people stop him?

Could it happen again? Do you think genocide—mass murder of a particular group of people—could take place in the United States?

Elie Wiesel lived through the Holocaust. His book Night *tells the powerful story of his experiences. Anne Frank died in the Holocaust, but the diary she kept before she died was preserved.* The Diary of a Young Girl *is a moving book about her experiences.* Night and Fog *is a short film (about 30 minutes) about the concentration camps in Europe during World War II. It is excellent, but very upsetting—definitely not for young children.*

Situation Desperate—but Not Hopeless!

In America, the early 1930s were like the morning after a bad fight. Americans had thought of themselves as "winners" in the 1920s. President Hoover had told them they were coming close to a "final triumph" over poverty. But after the stock market had crashed . . . after the banks had started to close . . . after millions of people had lost their jobs . . . Americans felt as if

Scenes like this were common during the Depression. Unemployed people had no money and nothing to do.

they'd taken a bad beating. They were losing the fight against poverty. And they hated feeling like losers.

As the hard times continued, more and more Americans just gave up hope. When the stock market crashed in 1929, a few people were so upset about the money they lost that they killed themselves by jumping from the windows of New York City skyscrapers. But that was nothing compared to 1931. That year, reported the Metropolitan Life Insurance Company, about 20,000 Americans committed suicide. Many people thought the United States was falling to pieces. In 1932, 32,000 new immigrants came to the United States – but 103,000 people *left* the country. The American Dream wasn't looking so good.

Turning Things Around

But not everyone gave up hope. In spite of their fear and anger, many Americans started reaching out to each other, trying to make things better.

Families moved in together to share the cost of food and housing. Housewives fed hungry people who came to their back doors looking for food. Churches, charity groups, and city governments opened soup kitchens. Millions of Americans waited in line every day for a little hot food. Free clinics offered basic medical care. In 1932, one railroad company even changed its rule banning homeless people from using empty freight cars as places to sleep. Instead of forcing the people to leave, the company added *extra* cars to help the homeless.

But all this "person-to-person" help wasn't enough. There were too many millions of people in trouble. The government would eventually have to put the country back to work. In the meantime, people led their lives.

PRICES DROP

Comparing prices in the 1920s and 1930s

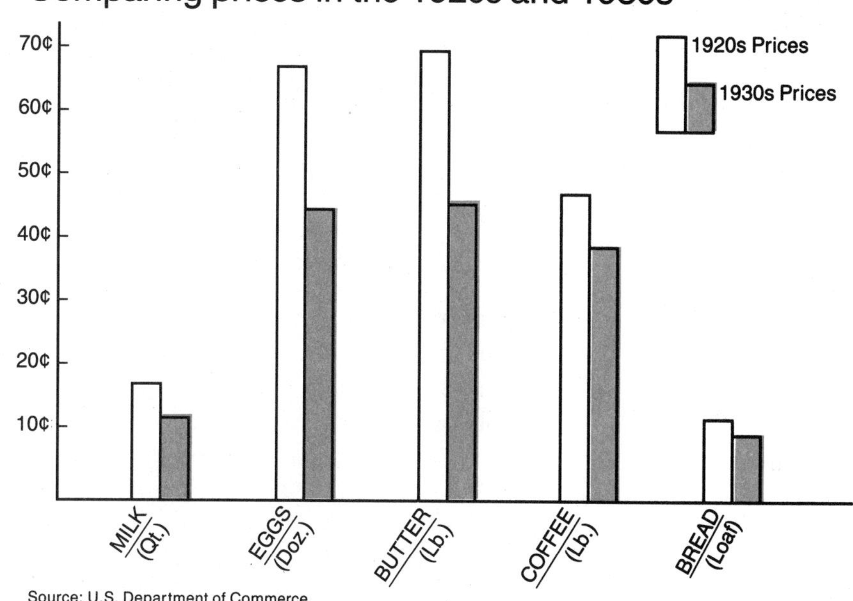

Source: U.S. Department of Commerce

In Their Own Words

Chicago writer Studs Terkel talked to hundreds of people who lived through the Depression years. He put their stories together in a book called *Hard Times*. Here are some of the voices of the Depression:

A teenager:

> I finished high school in 1930, and I walked out into this thing. . . . I was a big husky athlete, but there just wasn't any work. Already by that time, if you were looking for a job at a [gas station], you had to have a college degree. . . .
>
> I'd get up at five in the morning and head for the waterfront. Outside the Spreckles Sugar Refinery, outside the gates, there would be a thousand men. You know dang well there's only three or four jobs. The guy would come out with two little . . . cops: "I need two guys for the bull gang. Two guys to go into the hole." A thousand men would fight like a

The man on the right is selling apples on a New York City street corner. This was a common way for unemployed people to earn some money.

pack of Alaskan dogs to get through there.

A schoolgirl:

I remember all of a sudden we had to move. My father lost his job, and we moved into a double-garage. The landlord didn't charge us rent for seven years. We had a coal stove, and we had to each take turns, the three of us kids, to warm our legs. . . . In the morning, we'd get out and get some snow and put it on the stove and melt it and wash around our faces. . . . [We'd] put on two pairs of socks on each hand and two pairs of socks on our feet, and . . . off we'd walk, three, four miles to school.

My father had owned three or four homes. His father left them to him. He lost these one by one. . . . [But] my father was pretty sharp in a way. He always could get something to feed us kids. We lived about three months on candy cods; they're little chocolate square things. We had these melted in milk. And he had a part-time job in a Chinese restaurant. We lived on those fried noodles. I can't stand 'em today.

A college student:

One friend of mine came to college . . . [in] an old Model T

Songs of the Depression

Perhaps the most famous song of the era was "Brother, Can You Spare a Dime?" Its depressing lyrics were a good example of the bitter humor of the Depression. It seems to ask, "We fought a war for *this*?"

Once I built a railroad, made it run,
Made it race against time.
Once I built a railroad, now it's done.
Brother, can you spare a dime?
Say, don't you remember, they called me Al,
It was Al all the time?
Say, don't you remember, I'm your Pal!
Buddy, can you spare a dime?

Another song sang the blues of the sharecropper, who farmed land for rich owners. Most of the sharecropper's earnings went to the owner of the land. This song was sung in migrant labor camps in California:

Eleven cent cotton and forty cent meat
How in the world can a poor man eat?
Flour up high, cotton down low,
How in the world can you raise the dough?
Clothes worn out, shoes run down,
Old slouch hat with a hole in the crown. . . .

Ford Sedan, about a 1919 model. . . . He lived in it all year long. He cooked and slept and studied inside that Model T Ford Sedan. How he managed I will never know. I once went there for dinner. He cooked a pretty good one on a little stove he had in this thing. He was a brilliant student. I don't know where he is now, but I shouldn't be surprised if he's the head of some big corporation . . . Survival. . . .

Some [students] engaged in strange occupations. There was a biological company that would pay a penny apiece for cockroaches. They needed these in research, I guess. Some students went cockroach hunting every night.

A hobo:

Black and white, it didn't make any difference who you were, 'cause everybody was poor. . . .We used to take a big pot and cook food, cabbage, meat, and beans all together. We all set together, we made a tent. Twenty-five or thirty would be out on the side of the rail, white and colored. They didn't have no mothers or sisters, they didn't have no home, they were dirty, they had overalls on, they didn't have no food, they didn't have anything. . . .

The shame I was feeling. I walked out [on my family] because I didn't have a job. I said, "I'm goin' out in the world and get me a job." And God help me, I couldn't get anything. I wouldn't let them see me dirty and ragged and I hadn't shaved. I wouldn't send 'em no picture. ■

Check your local library for records by Woody Guthrie, Pete Seeger, Huddie ("Leadbelly") Ledbetter, Sonny Terry, and other blues singers and folksingers who began their careers during the Depression.

This restaurant window shows the low prices of the Depression. Many people could not afford to pay even these prices.

The Dust Bowl

A cloud of dust (right) rolls into Clayton, New Mexico. During the 1930s, dry weather turned the Great Plains states into a "dust bowl."

A Texas schoolboy remembers dust storms that buried towns and farms in the 1930s:

> These storms were like rolling black smoke. We had to keep the lights on all day. We went to school with headlights on, and with dust masks on. I saw a woman who thought the world was coming to an end. She dropped down on her knees in the middle of Main Street in Amarillo and prayed out loud: "Dear Lord! Please give them another chance."

By 1933, a lack of rain had turned the Great Plains into a "dust bowl." The land had become so dry that on just one windy day, thousands of tons of soil could be lifted up and blown away. Crops dried up in the fields – and farm families began to leave the land.

Most of them went west. They hoped to find jobs picking fruit and vegetables so they could earn money to buy farms in the rich green lands of California. Because many of them came from Oklahoma, they were nicknamed "Okies." Actually, though, they came from all over – Missouri, Arkansas, Texas, Kansas, and other states. Some walked. Others drove old cars. At times, there were so many people going west that their cars filled *both* sides of the highway.

Folksinger Woody Guthrie and others wrote songs about the thousands of Americans who "hit the road" in the 1930s:

I've been having some hard
traveling,
I thought you knowed
I've been having some hard
traveling
Way down the road. . . .
Mean old judge, he says to me,
It's ninety days for vagrancy,
And I've been hitting some hard
traveling, Lord.©

Lack of rain had turned the Great Plains into a "dust bowl."

Not the Promised Land

Most of the "hard travelers" did *not* find a better life in California. The owners of the big farms paid low wages because so many people were looking

Farm machinery at a South Dakota farm (below) is buried under dust.

Many farmers left the "dust bowl" for the West. This Texas family is on the road in the late 1930s.

for jobs. Families lived in run-down shacks and drank dirty water from ditches. After the fruit or vegetables were picked, the owners sometimes used guns or tear gas to force workers to move on. The workers could not buy land for themselves.

In 1937, the federal government began to help the traveling workers by supplying them with food, medical care, and simple housing. But life did not get better for many families until World War II created new jobs – in wartime factories or in the army. ■

The "Okies" were unhappy because they could farm only land owned by other people. They could not own land themselves. Migrant farm workers today have this problem – and others.

Do you think that migrant workers should be included in "minimum wage" and other laws that protect workers? Why or why not?

Should illegal immigrants be protected by U.S. laws? For example, should their children go to American schools for free?

From John Steinbeck's *The Grapes of Wrath*

The Grapes of Wrath is a novel about what life was like for the "Okies" who went west to California looking for work. It was published in 1939 and won a Pulitzer Prize in 1940. Here is a short "sample" of the book:

> The cars of the migrant people crawled out of the side roads on to the great cross-country highway, and they took the migrant way to the West. In the daylight they scuttled like bugs to the westward; and as the dark caught them, they clustered like bugs near to shelter and to water. And because they were lonely and perplexed, because they had all come from a place of sadness and worry and defeat, and because they were all going to a new mysterious place, they huddled together; they talked together; they shared their lives, their food, and the things they hoped for in the new country.

Fashion Statements

Do long skirts mean "hard times"? Nobody has ever proved it – but in the 1920s, 1930s, and 1940s, women's hemlines *did* seem to rise and fall with the economy.

In the 1920s, times were good. The stock market was up, and so were the skirt lengths of stylish women around the country. But when the stock market went down, so did the hemlines. During the Depression years, skirt lengths were well below the knees. What happened when World War II brought a wartime boom economy? You guessed it: hemlines went up again.

Of course, the short skirts of the war years *also* helped to save materials – cotton and wool that could be used for uniforms, tents, and other wartime products. The war changed fashion and fads in other ways too. Teenage boys wore recycled army boots and bomber jackets. Their mothers loved military-style hats and Eisenhower jackets modeled after General Eisenhower's uniform.

High school students weren't fighting in the war. But they developed "uniforms" of their own: baggy shirts, rolled-up blue jeans, and two-colored saddle shoes or loafers. One fashion trend gave a generation its name. Teenage girls of the 1940s were often called "bobby-soxers" – in honor of their favorite rolled-down socks. ■

As shown in the drawings, hemlines dipped in the 1930s (left) and then rose in the 1940s (above).

Bobby sox, army boots, and Eisenhower jackets were popular during World War II. What are some of the fashions that are popular today? What seems to make a style popular?

Some people think advertisers make young people want styles that cost too much money, such as expensive running shoes. Do you think fashion advertising should be controlled? If so, how?

War Effort at Home

Americans who stayed at home during World War II remember seeing signs like these:

> USE IT UP–
> WEAR IT OUT–
> MAKE IT DO!
> Our Labor and Our Goods Are Fighting
>
> UNCLE SAM NEEDS
> Your Discarded
> SILK AND NYLON STOCKINGS
> for Gun Powder Bags
> Please Launder and Leave HERE
>
> JUNK MAKES FIGHTING WEAPONS
> One old shovel
> will help make 4 hand grenades!

Life on the "home front" meant doing whatever you could to help the war effort. Some people grumbled – but most Americans wanted to help. Americans saved paper, tin foil, cooking fat, and rubber tires. They searched attics and basements for useful things: rusty baby buggies, old radiators, worn-out shoes, old rubber tires. Women knitted socks. It seemed as if *everybody* had planted a "victory garden" – a home garden that fed the family and made more farm-grown food available for soldiers. In 1943, there were more than 20 million of them. They produced at least one-third of all the vegetables eaten in the United States that year.

Everyone had ration books. These

New Yorkers (below) wait in line for war ration books.

controlled how much of a scarce item people could buy. There were ration books for gasoline, sugar, meat, coffee, butter, and many other products. "I remember all the neighborhood women sitting around the kitchen table pooling and trading ration coupons," one woman recalls. "My grandmother raised chickens, so we often didn't need our meat coupons. . . . [There was] a kind of . . . team spirit."

Entertaining "the Boys"

Saving tin cans was good for the war – but America wanted to do something for "the boys" in uniform too. Across the country, groups of volunteers opened clubs for servicemen. Many of them were run by the Red Cross or by a new volunteer group, the USO (United Service Organizations).

As the war went on, the USO became famous for bringing great traveling shows to soldiers and sailors fighting around the world. Hollywood stars of the day such as Bing Crosby,

An "A" card (left) allowed its owner to buy three gallons of gasoline a week. Silk and nylon stockings (below left) and waste paper (below right) were recycled into war supplies.

Because so many men were in the armed forces, nearly 20 million women had joined the work force by 1944.

Danny Kaye, and Ann Sheridan sang, danced, and joked with the troops – sometimes on stages only a few miles from the combat zone. A comedian named Bob Hope was a big hit.

For some women, wartime romances and marriages were the way to "do their bit" for the soldiers. In small towns and big cities, young women volunteered to work in local USO clubs. It was a romantic time. Soldiers and girls met, courted, and married – sometimes in just a few days.

"The social pressure for young women to marry soldiers was incredibly strong," one woman remembers. "It was in everything we did, everything we read, the songs we listened to on the radio, in movies. . . ." Another recalls that it was "a very hectic, exciting time. . . ." She remembers that "relationships were extremely intense, because you didn't know how long they would last."

THEN & NOW

Once Bob Hope started entertaining the troops overseas, he never stopped! Over the years, he visited U.S. troops in Korea, in Vietnam, and on U.S. Army bases and ships across the world. In 1990 – at age 87 – he took a show to Saudi Arabia, just before the Persian Gulf war began.

The Saudi Arabian show was a bit different from most of Hope's shows. Until then, beautiful women had always been a part of Hope's entertainments. But Hope had to think about the feelings of people in Saudi Arabia. In that strict Muslim nation, people would not have liked women to perform in public – especially if they wore "revealing" clothes. So Hope made some changes in his usual show, and everyone was satisfied.

Rosie the Riveter

"For the first time in my life, I found out that I could do something with my hands besides bake a pie," remembers a woman who went to work in a factory during the war. By 1944, nearly 20 million women were in the work force. Some of them had worked before the war – but many women were doing their first paid work. The government wanted women to work and created posters to push the idea: "My husband's in the Army," said one. "I'm in a shipyard. . . . We're in the war together."

Where did women work? In shipyards, in airplane and truck factories, in lumber mills, and on docks. Women learned to be mechanics, welders, crane operators, bus drivers, and gas station attendants.

Cowgirls herded cattle, and "lumberjills" cut trees. And they were getting paid. For many American women, wartime jobs were a first taste of the power to earn money.

Americans liked artist Norman Rockwell's drawings of "Rosie the Riveter"—a strong, muscular young woman in overalls. But many people felt it wasn't really "nice" for women to do men's jobs. After the war ended, some factories fired their women workers. The country told women it was time to go back home, bake cookies, and have babies.

But the war work changed many American women forever. "The war years offered new possibilities," says one woman. "You came out to California, put on your pants, and took your lunch pail to a man's job. . . . This was the beginning of women's feeling that they could do something more." ■

Would today's Americans be willing to give up things for a war effort? Would they be willing to grow their own food? To save things and then send them to "the boys"? To use ration books? Why or why not?

Pretend you are a woman who worked in a factory during World War II. You enjoyed working and earning money. Now the war is over, and you have been fired. You are expected to go back home and let a man take your job. Write a diary entry saying how you feel about all of this—and what your hopes are for the future.

Libraries have books of paintings by American artist Norman Rockwell. He understood the feelings of wartime America well—not just in "Rosie the Riveter," but in many paintings. His Four Freedoms *show what Americans felt "the boys" were fighting for. You may enjoy looking at his paintings.*

This butcher shop counter displays prices and ration point values.

Escapes

It's the 1930s. Many Americans are out of work. No one has much money. People make ends meet – barely – with the help of an occasional bag of groceries from a charity. They live in small apartments, sharing them with a few relatives and another family. In the meantime, they hear on the radio that the storm clouds of war are gathering in Europe.

But life is not all gloom. People still like to laugh and have a good time. Maybe fun is needed more than ever in bad times. Americans need to *escape* – and they find ways.

Fun for All

If you could afford to spend a dime, you could buy a magazine or comic book: *Buck Rogers* for children, *Screenland* for movie watchers, *Amazing Stories* for science fiction fans. In the early 1930s, a dime got you into the movies for an afternoon. You could even have fun if all you could afford to spend was a nickel. In the mid-1930s, a nickel bought a double-dip ice cream cone or a game of bingo at a church carnival.

There was fun for everyone. Miniature golf was a national craze. People spent hours trying to hit a golf ball around a tiny golf course – complete with castles, windmills, and sand traps. Dancing was more popular than ever. Teenagers liked to jitterbug. This was a dance in which couples made acrobatic steps and swings while holding hands. Sometimes the boy lifted his partner high in the air. Among other dance crazes were the conga and the big apple. To do the conga, a group of dancers formed a

Soldiers and civilians form a conga line to celebrate the end of World War II.

Bingo was another popular escape during the Depression.

long, snaky line and danced around the room with their hands on one another's hips. The big apple ended with the dancers raising their arms high and shouting, "Praise Allah!" ■

During the Depression, people learned to "make their own fun" with dancing and simple games. Do people make their own fun today—or does all entertainment have to be "packaged" for them? What kinds of fun do today's children have? How does it compare with the fun you had as a child?

THEN & NOW

When people of the 1930s went to the movies for escape, they could *really* escape. Movie theaters weren't just theaters in those days. They were picture palaces. Some theaters were done in the style of Spanish villages—with a sky (the ceiling) full of stars (tiny lights)! Other theaters looked like Egyptian pyramids, Chinese palaces, or European opera houses. Theater lobbies often had crystal chandeliers, Oriental rugs, and antique furniture. People enjoyed these things. Even the poorest person could feel rich in the luxurious surroundings.

Many of these picture palaces have been torn down. Today, most Americans see movies in the bare, boxy rooms of a multiscreen theater at a mall.

The new theaters are probably more practical. And movie prices are high enough today without viewers having to pay for upkeep on a palace. But the old theaters were magic!

At the Movies

Movies were the favorite kind of escape for Depression-weary Americans. They helped people forget the real world. Even if people in the audience didn't have fancy clothes to wear, they liked to see movie actors dress up: Ginger Rogers in silk and feathers, Fred Astaire in top hat and white tie. Director Busby Berkeley's musicals about show business had songs, dances, and great costumes. "Screwball" comedies like *Bringing Up Baby* and *My Man Godfrey* were popular. In screwball stories, the hero and heroine were usually rich – and their troubles were funny, not serious. The rich were often shown to be foolish in these movies. The poor enjoyed laughing at them.

A scene from the musical *Gold Diggers of 1933* (above) by director Busby Berkeley. This movie theater (right) shows the luxury of "picture palaces" of the 1930s.

Fred Astaire and Ginger Rogers (above), and Bette Davis (below) are examples of 1930s movie stars.

The Movie Business

As much as people liked movies, however, moviemakers had reason to be scared in the early 1930s. The Depression was hurting the movie business. Numbers told the story: In 1930, 90 million people saw a movie in the United States in an average week. In 1931, as the Depression took hold, the number fell to 75 million. In both 1932 and 1933, it was 60 million. Almost 5,000 movie theaters closed in the first half of the 1930s.

How did Hollywood respond? Movie producers worked hard to sell their product. The "double feature"–two movies for the price of one–was one way they filled seats. Producers and theater owners also arranged "giveaways" at theaters, and lucky customers went home with such things as dishes and encyclopedias. To save money, filmmakers also shortened the time it took to produce a movie. Some films were made in just a few weeks. Filmmakers also started what became known as the "star system." Popular actors such as Clark Gable, Bette Davis, and James Cagney turned out

Make-Believe

What were the audiences seeing in the 1930s? Walt Disney produced some of his greatest cartoons, including *Snow White and the Seven Dwarfs* in 1937 and *Pinocchio* in 1939. Disney combined creative drawing and strong characters to please audiences of all ages.

Also in 1939, *The Wizard of Oz* came to the big screen. One of the first movies in color, it has been delighting viewers ever since.

Gone With the Wind, an extremely popular film based on a novel about the Civil War, is a third famous movie that came out in 1939. In a way, *Gone With the Wind* also was an escape. People preferred to cry over a long-ago

***Gone With the Wind*, starring Clark Gable and Vivien Leigh, was one of the most popular films that Hollywood ever made.**

film after film for the same studio. The studios knew that people liked these stars and supported their stars with publicity campaigns.

These strategies worked for the movie industry. By 1935, the weekly audience was back up to 75 million. A 1936 survey showed that more than 50 percent of the American public saw more than one movie a month, and almost 25 percent saw at least one a week. Only 16 percent said that they *never* saw a movie.

war rather than worry about the one that was coming.

But by far the biggest money-maker was Shirley Temple. She was a curly-haired little girl whose bright smile captured millions of hearts. At age six, she danced and sang in *Stand Up and Cheer*—a 1934 movie musical that told Americans they *could* survive hard times. Shirley made 35 movies in the 1930s. She often played the part of a poor child, or an orphan, or a child caught in a war. But she always survived—and so did her happy smile. She made moviegoers believe that if Shirley could make it, so could America.

Public Enemies?

Gangsters and monsters were big stars of Depression-era movies too. James Cagney starred in *Public Enemy,* Paul Muni starred as a Capone-like gangster in the original *Scarface*, and Edward G. Robinson was Rico, a vicious gangster, in *Little Caesar*. Boris Karloff played the monster in *Frankenstein*—and a 16-inch gorilla doll played the giant ape in *King Kong*.

What was the attraction? Why did movie audiences like to see King Kong tear up New York City skyscrapers? Why did they like to watch gangsters shoot up the town? One answer is that during the Depression, people were very angry about what was happening in the world. Gangster and monster movies gave people a safe way to "let off steam." Another answer is that they made people feel as if they were in control. At a time when the world seemed to be upside down, people could pretend they were like the powerful characters in the movies. ■

What do you think about today's super-violent movies and TV shows? Do they give audiences a healthy way to get rid of anger and frustration, like the gangster and monster movies of the 1930s—or do they serve a different purpose? Why do you think these movies and shows are so popular today?

Shirley Temple (above) in one of the many movies she starred in during the 1930s. King Kong (below) tears up New York City. The giant ape was really a 16-inch doll.

Comedy's Golden Age

The Marx Brothers (above) in *Duck Soup*. Vaudeville stars W. C. Fields and Mae West (above right) in *My Little Chickadee*.

Vaudeville fans of the 1930s liked to say that movies and radio were killing vaudeville. But vaudeville – the live, traveling stage shows of the early 1900s – wasn't really dead. In the 1930s, many great vaudeville performers found that radio shows and movies made them even *bigger* stars than before.

Experienced stars such as W.C. Fields, Bob Hope, and Jack Benny made the change from vaudeville to radio. So did some great comedy teams, including George Burns and his wife, Gracie Allen, and Abbott and Costello. And who would have thought that a vaudeville ventriloquist could be a radio star? Edgar Bergen made his wooden dummy, Charlie McCarthy, "talk" – but on radio, who could tell if Bergen's lips were moving? No one seemed to mind.

Moviemakers liked to hire vaudeville stars because they could do just about anything: dance, sing, tell jokes, even juggle. Among the many movie stars of the 1930s who started in vaudeville were the Marx Brothers, Laurel and Hardy, Mickey Rooney, and Mae West. And all the stars of *The Wizard of Oz* – Judy Garland, Ray Bolger, Bert Lahr, Jack Haley, Billie Burke, and Frank Morgan – came from the vaudeville stage. ■

Swing, Swing, Swing

Have you ever noticed that each era seems to have its own "sound"—the "in" music that everyone listens to? Nowadays, rap music is popular. The sound of America in the late 1930s and early 1940s was "swing." Swing wasn't really new. It was jazz—the same kind of jazz music that black groups had played back in the 1920s. But in the 1930s, band leaders added plenty of saxophones, clarinets, and trumpets and sold their Big Band swing sound to a new generation of Americans.

Teenagers and adults waited for their favorite Big Band to come through town. Great band leaders were as well known as movie stars: Duke Ellington, Benny Goodman, Tommy and Jimmy Dorsey, Count Basie, Woody Herman, Kay Kyser, Glenn Miller. And for the first time, black and white musicians frequently played together on the same stage.

Above all else, swing music was for dancing. In the Swing Era, big ballrooms across the country were filled every Friday and Saturday night. Teenagers put nickels in jukeboxes and

Duke Ellington's band (left) onstage in 1943. Ellington is at the piano. Tommy Dorsey (below, on trombone) rehearses with his band.

The "King of Swing," Benny Goodman.

danced in the aisles of hamburger joints or ice cream parlors. And during World War II, a soldier on leave liked to look for a pretty girl – and a place to dance.

Today, jazz is just one part of American music. But for a few years in the 1930s and 1940s, the sound of "swingin' " jazz was the sound of America having fun. ■

The "swing" sound is still available in the recordings department of your local library. Music by Duke Ellington, Benny Goodman, Glenn Miller, and others should be there, so treat yourself to the sound of the 1930s.

The King and the Duke

The Big Bands of swing had their own "royal family." Bandleader Benny Goodman was called the "King of Swing." Another "royal" bandleader was "Duke" Ellington.

Benny Goodman

Benny Goodman (1909–1986) came from a Jewish immigrant family. He played with many bands in Chicago and New York during the 1920s. But by the 1930s, Goodman was tired of the sweet jazz that bands were playing for white audiences. He wanted a different sound – a hot sound.

Goodman met a black bandleader named Fletcher Henderson. Henderson's songs had the kind of sound Goodman wanted. When Henderson's band broke up because of money trouble, Goodman hired him. And when Goodman's band played Henderson's songs, crowds went wild. Benny Goodman had his hot sound.

Goodman was a skilled clarinetist. He also was a good judge of musical talent. He found great solo players to thrill the crowds. Audiences were still enjoying his music long after the Swing Era was over.

Duke Ellington

Edward Kennedy Ellington (1899–1974) was a jazz piano player in the 1920s. In the early 1930s, he was the bandleader at the famous Cotton Club in Harlem. A 1932 Ellington song may have given swing its name; one of its lines went, "It don't mean a thing if it ain't got that swing."

Ellington liked to write music that showed off the players in his band. "Duke plays the piano, but his real instrument is his band," a friend once said. Even as other styles of music grew in popularity, Ellington and the band kept creating and performing. Like Goodman, Duke Ellington showed that swing was here to stay.

Words of Protest

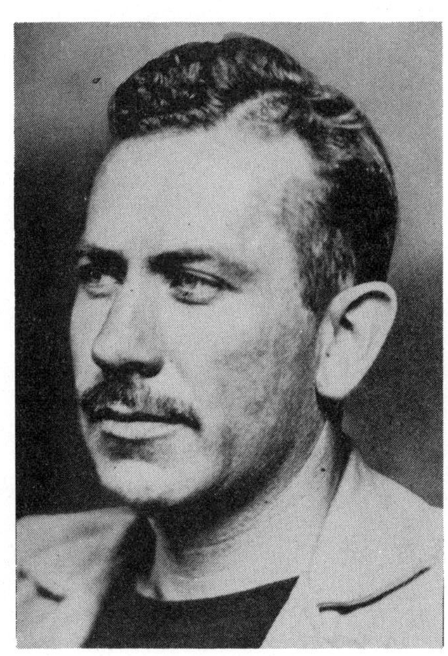

Richard Wright (left), James T. Farrell (center), and John Steinbeck (right) wrote about the injustices they saw in America.

Hard times made some Americans look for ways to forget their troubles. But some of America's best novelists, playwrights, and moviemakers wanted to talk about what was happening in America and the world – the bad as well as the good. During the Depression, important new books, plays, and movies took a hard look at the American Dream – and said the country needed to change.

Some writers thought their main purpose was to change America. These artists wanted to look at real life and talk about ways to fight injustice, poverty, and other social problems. Writers with these goals met at the first U.S. Writers' Congress in 1935.

One of the writers who attacked social problems in his novels was James T. Farrell. He was most famous for his trilogy (set of three novels) about a young Irish-American named Studs Lonigan. At the beginning of the first novel, *Young Lonigan*, 15-year-old Studs says to himself, "Well, I'm kissin' the old dump goodbye." He is referring to the grammar school that he is about to graduate from. In a larger sense, though, he is hoping to leave behind his lower-class, big-city neighborhood and its violent way of life. The trilogy shows his failure to build a better life.

Richard Wright looked at racial prejudice in his book *Native Son*. This novel gave many white readers their first look at the sufferings of American blacks. In its famous first scene, young Bigger Thomas defends his family from a large rat; finally, he kills the rat with a skillet. *Native Son* goes on to tell the story of Bigger's life of crime. In this novel and others, Wright showed that poverty, crime, and racism are related.

Novelist John Steinbeck wrote the most famous book about the hard times of the 1930s. In *The Grapes of Wrath*, Steinbeck wrote about an

A scene from a Group Theatre play.

Oklahoma family who lose their farm and travel to California hoping to make a new life for themselves. They find work picking fruit and vegetables. But the Joad family *doesn't* find a better life. Farm owners treat them cruelly. They work long hours for little pay. They are lost in the world – without a home, money, or protection. Like other writers of the times, Steinbeck used his work to wake people up. He wanted people to think about injustice.

Some theater groups and playwrights also tried to make audiences think about the need for change. The Group Theatre produced plays in New York City from 1931 to 1941. Its writers, directors, and actors used their work to point out injustices in American society. Probably the most famous playwright who wrote for the Group Theatre was Clifford Odets. His *Waiting for Lefty* was performed for the first time in 1935. It was based on a cabdrivers' strike that had occurred the year before. A look at a bit of dialogue from *Lefty* gives an idea of its style. Joe is complaining that people think he is "red" – Communist – just because he wants a fair contract:

> *Joe:* You boys know me. I ain't a red boy one bit. Here I'm carryin' a shrapnel that big I picked up in the war. And maybe I don't know it when it rains! Don't tell me red! You know what we are? The black and blue boys! We been kicked around so long we're black and blue from head to toes. But I guess anyone who says straight out he don't like it, he's a red boy to the leaders of the union. What's this crap about going home to hot suppers? I'm asking to your faces how many's got hot suppers to go to? Anyone who's sure of his next meal, raise your hand! . . . And that's why we're talking strike – to get a living wage!

Did most Americans read these books or see these plays? No. But the same ideas about social change turned up in popular movies. Millions of Americans saw the movie version of *The Grapes of Wrath*. Movies like director Frank Capra's *Meet John Doe* pictured big business as evil. In his work, Capra – like many writers and other artists of the time – showed ordinary Americans changing the world by working together to solve problems. ■

Many writers in the 1930s wanted to use their skill to change America – especially to fight poverty and injustice. Do you think this is what books are for? Or are they supposed to entertain people? How can a book entertain and also try to change the country? Have you ever read any books or seen any movies that do both?

ART DECO

If swing was the sound of the 1930s, Art Deco was the "look" of the decade. Most Americans of the 1930s didn't have money to buy Art Deco furniture. But they liked the way it looked in the movies or in magazine articles about rich people.

The Art Deco style was modern. Art Deco designers said that yesterday's furniture and buildings were too fancy and old-fashioned. They wanted to make a new style with simple, straight lines. They used modern materials: plastic, steel, concrete. Many of the designers borrowed ideas from modern art or from Native American designs. The Art Deco look turned up in everything from apartment buildings to chairs, from lamps to teapots. You can still see it in the architecture of cities that grew in the 1930s – Miami, for example.

Moviemakers of the 1930s liked the new look too. If you've seen Fred Astaire–Ginger Rogers dance movies, you've seen Art Deco: sharp, hard lines . . . strong blacks and whites . . . shiny metal tubes. For Americans of the Depression, the Art Deco style was the look of glamour and wealth. ■

Find out if any Art Deco–style buildings still stand in your town. The local historical society will know. Perhaps you can arrange an "Art Deco tour" of your town for family and friends.

The Art Deco look is shown in the architecture of this Miami building (above) and in its furniture (left).

Wartime Baseball

"They're Either Too Young or Too Old" was a popular song of the World War II era. It was about the lack of men available for romance during World War II. But it could just as easily have been about major-league baseball players.

Judge Kenesaw Mountain Landis, the commissioner of baseball, asked President Roosevelt if baseball should close down for the war. Roosevelt answered that baseball should continue; it would be good for the country's mood. But great players like Ted Williams, Joe DiMaggio, and Bob Feller were in the armed services. With many players in the war, teams had to struggle to fill their rosters. So they tried different ways.

Wanted: Players

In 1944, for example, the Chicago White Sox brought 35-year-old Roy Schalk out of retirement to play second base. He had last played in the majors in 1932. They expected to pair him with 37-year-old Luke Appling at shortstop. Third baseman Tony Cuccinello was also 37. Then Appling went into the service, and a player

A shortage of good players during the war resulted in many unlikely players making the majors. One-armed outfielder Pete Gray played 77 games for the St. Louis Browns in 1945.

young enough to be his son – 18-year-old Cass Michaels – took his place.

Except for Michaels, every man on the Sox infield was more than 30 years old. And three Sox pitchers were "old" as well, at ages 35, 39, and 41. They finished in seventh place.

The Cincinnati Reds went to the other extreme. One day in 1944, they brought in a 15-year-old pitcher named Joe Nuxhall to face the Chicago Cubs. After the Cubs scored seven runs in the first inning, Nuxhall was taken out of the game. Eight years later, he returned to the Reds and had a fine career.

The St. Louis Browns permitted a one-armed man – Pete Gray – to play the outfield. His right arm had been removed after a childhood accident, so he batted with his left hand. After catching a batted ball, he flipped it in front of his face, like a juggler. Then he would tuck his glove under his right armpit, snatch the ball out of the air, and throw it. Gray played in 77 games for the Browns in 1945.

Some teams brought back players who had not been good enough to make the team years before. Sigmund Jakucki had pitched briefly and unsuccessfully in the majors in 1936. He was brought back to the majors in 1944 and won 13 games for the Browns.

Judged by normal major-league standards, baseball teams were filled with the very old, the very young, and the very average. As you can imagine, the quality of play was not very good. In fact, it had never been worse.

But the fans didn't mind; they still came out to see the games. President Roosevelt was right; baseball *was* good for the country's mood.

"Neither Team Will Win"

Perhaps the low point of wartime baseball was the 1945 World Series. The war was over by then, but the players who had been in the armed forces weren't yet playing again. The series matched the two league champions: the Chicago Cubs and the Detroit Tigers. The Tigers' starting lineup was very old, and so were the Cubs' starting pitchers. One sportswriter watched the two teams practice before the series began. They played so badly that he jokingly predicted, "Neither team will win." (The Tigers finally did, shading the Cubs four games to three.)

By the next season, the players who had been in the war were back. The overly old, overly young, and less talented players had to find other jobs, but they had known all along that this would happen. Baseball had survived the war and was better than ever. ■

Judge Landis, longtime commissioner of baseball, opens another season by throwing out the first ball.

Major-league baseball was willing to shut down during World War II. Only President Roosevelt kept the baseball seasons from being canceled. If there were a big war today, do you think big-time sports would offer to shut down? Do you think many players would join the armed forces? Why or why not?

U.S. Gold in Berlin

In 1936, the Summer Olympic Games were held in Berlin, Germany. Germany's Nazi government wanted to use the Olympics to show the world the strength of the German "master race." Dictator Adolf Hitler was confident that the games would prove Germanic athletes were the best in the world. Nazi officials called blacks "nonhumans." But an African-American track star named Jesse Owens ruined Hitler's plans.

Owens was born in Danville, Alabama, the 10th and youngest child of a poor farmer. Even as a junior high school student, he was recognized as a brilliant sprinter. At a track meet during his sophomore year in college in 1935, Owens broke three world records and tied a fourth – all within one hour.

At the Berlin games, Owens won three individual gold medals – for the 100-meter dash, the 200-meter dash, and the long jump. Plus, he was part of the winning U.S. 400-meter relay team (four runners going 100 meters each).

The huge Olympic stadium echoed with the roar of the crowd chanting

Jesse Owens runs for the gold in the 400-meter relay. He won four gold medals in the 1936 Olympics.

"JESS-SEE O-WENS." But Hitler, who watched the events from his special box, reportedly stopped inviting gold medal winners to his box rather than have to congratulate black Americans.

Hitler had already snubbed two other black U.S. athletes. Cornelius Johnson and David Albritton had finished first and second in the high jump on the first afternoon of the games. Hitler left the stadium rather than shake their hands.

Two other black athletes placed second behind Owens in the dashes. One was Ralph Metcalfe, who later became an Illinois representative in the U.S. Congress. The other was Mark Robinson. His brother, Jackie Robinson, later became the first black to play major-league baseball.

The Germans failed to make the games a showcase for their "superior race." Maybe that is why they did their part to make sure there would be no Olympics in 1940 or 1944. Because of World War II, the Olympic tradition was broken in those years. The games did not resume until the winter of 1948, in Switzerland–after Nazi Germany had been defeated. ■

The Olympic torch arrives at the Berlin Olympics. The Nazis hoped to prove that white athletes were the best.

Joe Louis: Boxing's Best

It seemed that all of America sat next to the radio on June 22, 1938 – except for the 70,000 boxing fans crammed into New York's Yankee Stadium. All were following one of the biggest boxing matches in the sport's history. It was a rematch between German boxer Max Schmeling and world heavyweight champion Joe Louis.

Two years earlier, Schmeling had handed Louis his first defeat as a professional boxer. The German had been cheered on by many white Americans who thought of the fight primarily as a match between a white man and a black man. These fans were pleased when Louis lost in the 12th round.

By the time the rematch was arranged in 1938, Louis had defeated Jim Braddock to become world heavyweight champion, and many Americans had turned against Germany because of Adolf Hitler. Two minutes into the fight, Schmeling lay on the canvas. Louis was the clear winner, and this time, Americans celebrated by dancing in the streets.

Joe Louis (below) took only two minutes to knock out Max Schmeling in their 1938 title fight. Babe Didrikson (far right) throwing the javelin; she excelled in every sport that she tried.

Louis was called the "Brown Bomber" with good reason. In his 17 years as a professional boxer, he won 68 times and lost just three. Fifty-four of the wins were knockouts. He was heavyweight champion for 12 years, from 1937 until his retirement in 1949.

Louis, the seventh of eight children, was born to a poor family in Alabama in 1914. Joe's family moved to Detroit when he was 12 years old. Joe worked on an auto assembly line, as his father had done.

When Louis began to box, he was lucky to have good managers. One of their pieces of advice to him was this: "After you beat a white opponent, don't smile." Sadly, it was good advice for a black fighter in the 1930s. Louis worked hard to show no emotion.

It was true that blacks were unwelcome in most sports. But Joe Louis was treated like a hero. He was the first black fighter to be accepted by white America. ■

You can find out more about Joe Louis, Jesse Owens, and other black stars of the 1936 Olympics in A Hard Road to Glory, *by Arthur Ashe. The book tells the story of African-American athletes in the United States. Ashe was a top professional tennis player in the 1960s and 1970s.*

Babe Didrikson: Versatile Champion

"I've decided I want to be a lady now," said Babe Didrikson. She was apologizing for canceling a boxing match with a (male) heavyweight.

Boxing wasn't the only so-called "man's activity" that Mildred "Babe" Didrikson tried. She once threw a baseball 296 feet to win a national contest. In an exhibition baseball game, she struck out Joe DiMaggio.

Almost a baby, just 19 years old in the Los Angeles Olympics of 1932, Didrikson won gold medals in the hurdles and javelin throw. She would have won another in the high jump but was disqualified for diving over the bar. This style was later approved for high jumping.

Babe Didrikson excelled in every sport she tried. She was good at tennis, bowling, fencing, skating, shooting, cycling, billiards, and handball. She even put on pads and a helmet and practiced with the Southern Methodist University football team.

Later in life, she took up golf and won championships in England and the United States. She was confident and bold, even when she competed against men (which was somewhat unusual for the times). In golf, the player who wins one hole tees off first for the next one. A man, thinking that he would do the gentlemanly thing, once offered Didrikson the choice of being first on the opening tee.

"You better hit first," she said, "because it's the last time you'll get the honor." ■

FOOTBALL DIGS IN

The Rose Bowl seats more than 100,000.

During the Depression and the war years, football began to come into its own as a major American spectator sport. Both the college game and the professional game gained millions of fans.

Bowls of Plenty

By the 1930s, Saturday afternoons in the autumn were *football* afternoons in America's university towns. College football captured the nation's attention. This was because fans were thrilled by teams led by great college coaches: "Pop" Warner of the Carlisle Indian School, Amos Alonzo Stagg of the University of Chicago, and Knute Rockne of Notre Dame. Interest in the game grew too, as fans argued about changes in rules and strategies. But college football's popularity was also due to an idea whose time had come in the 1930s – the postseason "bowl" game.

Since early in the century, the New Year's Day Rose Bowl has been played in Pasadena, California. In 1933, the city of Miami, Florida, invited the University of Miami and Manhattan College to play in a game called the Orange Bowl. In 1935, Tulane and Temple met in the first Sugar Bowl in

THEN & NOW

The Big Four bowl games continue – the Rose, Cotton, Orange, and Sugar bowls. More and more new bowls are added all the time, however. There are now more than 24 postseason bowl games. Some fans think that the newer ones don't have much tradition behind them and that they take attention away from the older bowls. Others say that tradition develops only over time – and that a few great games will make the California, Freedom, and Holiday bowls as big as their older brothers in future years.

New Orleans, Louisiana. Two years later, Dallas, Texas, hosted Marquette and Texas Christian in the Cotton Bowl. America's sports fans now had new events to look forward to every year.

Fit to a T

Meanwhile, the National Football League was also establishing itself. There's a line in the Chicago Bears' fight song that goes, "We'll never forget the way you thrilled the nation / with your T formation." It was true; professional football, with athletes who were paid to suit up and play the game, was thrilling millions. Pro football was becoming a major sport in the United States in the 1930s.

The excitement created by the T formation – a new way to line up the team that had the ball – was just part of the reason why pro football grew more popular in the decade. Changes in rules and ideas for ways to move or defend the ball, some taken from college football, gave the game more scoring and added skill to it. Teams moved to bigger cities and larger stadiums, which meant that more people could come to watch games. Smart team owners added crowd-pleasing halftime shows, complete with colorful marching bands. Great stars began to play pro football, including quarterbacks Sammy Baugh, Don Hutson, and Sid Luckman. And there were many memorable games for fans to enjoy watching or listening to on the radio.

One of the most memorable was the championship game of 1940. The Bears and the Washington Redskins had finished first in their divisions and were set to play for the championship. It was expected to be a close game. The Bears had the T formation going rather well that day. Final score: Bears 73, Skins 0. It may have been painful for Washington fans, but it was great for pro football. Everyone talked about the game for weeks. And pro football was on its way to challenging baseball for the title "The National Game." ■

What changes have occurred in NFL rules during the past few years? Do you think they have helped or hurt the game?

Coach George Halas talking with his Chicago Bears during the 1935 football season.

The Luckiest Man Alive

On the Fourth of July, 1939, baseball hero Lou Gehrig stood under blue skies in a packed Yankee Stadium and spoke into a microphone: "Today I think I am the luckiest man alive." Gehrig, the "Iron Horse" who had thrilled baseball fans for 15 seasons, was quitting the game. He was too ill to play.

But that day, Gehrig Appreciation Day, the fans let out a deafening roar as he spoke to the crowd of 60,000. "You've been reading about my bad break for weeks now. But I have much to live for."

Lou Gehrig in action. The Yankees' "Iron Horse" set a baseball record by playing in 2,130 straight games.

Lou Gehrig fights back tears on Gehrig Appreciation Day in July 1939.

Lou Gehrig was one of baseball's best players. The New York Yankees' first baseman was a hitter and fielder of great skill. He was known as the "Iron Horse" because he never missed a game. In fact, he had played in 2,130 straight Yankee games. No other player has ever approached this record. He was a two-time winner of the American League's MVP (most valuable player) award.

The Yankees won the American League pennant eight times during Lou's 15 seasons. Lou led or tied the league in home runs three times and in RBIs (runs batted in) four times.

Lou Gehrig came from humble beginnings. His parents had immigrated to New York from Germany. They wanted their children to have a better education than they had. They were proud when Lou became a student at Columbia University. His success with the Yankees made them even prouder.

Tragedy and Grace

When people remember Lou Gehrig, however, it is with sadness as well as pride. This is because Gehrig died young. In June of 1939, doctors found that the 36-year-old Gehrig had a rare disease, amyotrophic lateral sclerosis (ALS). This is an illness that causes the muscles to weaken over time. It is always fatal. Toward the end, a person with ALS can barely move.

On June 2, 1941, less than two years after his disease was diagnosed, Lou Gehrig died. ALS is now often called "Lou Gehrig's disease" after its most famous victim. Scientists and fund-raising groups are working to find a cure for this killer. The memory of Lou Gehrig helps to inspire them. ■

You can find out more about ALS by writing to the Amyotrophic Lateral Sclerosis Association at 21021 Ventura Blvd., Suite 321, Woodland Hills, CA 91364. ALSA will be happy to send fact sheets on the disease if you send a stamped, self-addressed envelope.

The Pride of the Yankees *is a 1942 movie about the life of Lou Gehrig. It stars Gary Cooper, a popular film actor of the 1940s and 1950s, as Gehrig. It should be available at any large video rental store or your local library.*

Causes of the Great Depression

Life is made up of patterns. People's lives go from birth to old age. The four seasons follow one another during the year. A nation's economy also has a pattern – of ups and downs.

Before the Industrial Revolution – when people began using machines to manufacture goods – ups and downs depended on such things as the weather. If too much rain fell, for example, crops died, and the economy was in bad shape. Since the Industrial Revolution, however, the economy has become much more complicated. So have the reasons for its ups and downs.

Economists do not agree about what caused the Great Depression of the 1930s. But they believe the following played at least some part.

• Farmers: Farmers were producing too much food. They had expanded production during World War I, when the demand overseas for food was very high. To expand production, farmers had taken out loans to buy more land and new equipment. After the war, however, the British and the French returned to growing their own food. As a result, American farmers could no longer sell their crops in Europe. But they still had to pay off their loans and taxes.

• Factories: Factories built after World War I used more machines run by fewer workers. The machines were very efficient. But machines do not buy goods. Fewer workers meant fewer people with money to buy the goods the machines turned out.

• Buying on time: Before the 1920s, Americans paid cash for whatever they bought. After World War I, however, industry found itself with huge amounts of goods to sell. To make it easier for people to pay for goods, industry came up with the idea of the installment plan, or "buying on credit."

By 1929, millions of Americans were deeply in debt. They could no longer afford to buy goods.

• An income gap: Income was distributed unevenly. The rich were very rich, and the poor were very poor. In 1920, for example, a coal miner earned $10 a week. That same year, automobile manufacturer Henry Ford paid an income tax of $2.6 million. More important, about half the nation's families earned less than they needed for a decent life. Most people could barely afford one outfit of clothes a year. Many had no electricity in their homes. If wages had been higher, people could have bought more.

Economists usually sum this up as "overproduction and under-consumption." In other words, farms and factories turn out more goods than people can afford to buy. To cure this kind of depression, economists say, you have to create a better balance between what people produce and what they consume. ■

Many uprooted families from the plains moved to California to work. This child, dragging a cotton sack, is ready to work in the field.

A Bank "Holiday"

One day, you go to your bank. You find a big, noisy crowd of people there. They are all pressing against the teller windows, desperately trying to get their money out of the bank. What do you do?

If this had happened during the four months before FDR became president, you probably would have joined the crowd. Why? Because there was a banking crisis in the country. Banks had also been feeling the effects of the Depression. Like millions of investors, they had lost money in the stock market crash. And they continued to lose money because businesses, farmers, and homeowners could not pay back their loans or take out new ones. A rumor began to spread that banks had no cash left. At once, all of those with a checking or a savings account rushed to their bank to take their money out. The rumor was not true. But it was very harmful just the same. Banks do not keep on hand all the money that people have put in their accounts. Instead, they invest most of it. As a result, if all account owners try to take their money out at the same time, the bank does not have enough cash on hand to pay them.

A bank run in progress. The state of New Jersey later closed this bank.

Preventing "bank runs" was one of FDR's first jobs. Two days after taking office, he called for a bank "holiday." Every bank in the United States was closed. Experts then examined bank records to see whether banks were in good financial shape. By the end of the month, three out of four banks had reopened their doors. The rest failed the test and were closed.

FDR's plan worked. When the banks reopened, people had confidence in them again.

Bank Reform

A bank holiday was good for a week or two, but what would protect depositors from losing their savings in the future? One answer was the Federal Deposit Insurance Corporation, commonly known as the FDIC. The FDIC, which was formed in June of 1933, insures bank accounts. If a bank goes out of business, the federal government makes sure its account owners do not lose their money. In 1933, the FDIC insured accounts up to $2,500. In 1991, it insured accounts up to $100,000. ■

Some people say the Social Security system should be voluntary—that is, people could choose whether or not to be part of it. If you didn't contribute part of your pay, you wouldn't get money from the system after you stopped working. On the other hand, you could use the money you did not contribute to invest in stocks or real estate. Would you be in favor of changing Social Security in this way? Why or why not?

In 1900, about 4 percent of the American people were age 65 or older. By the year 2000, about 12 percent will be in that age group. What effects do you think this will have on the nation's economy?

Three Isms

Have you ever decided not to buy something because the price was too high? Or turned down a job because the pay was too low? You can do this because the United States has an economic system called *capitalism.*

Capitalism

Under capitalism, the economy is controlled mostly by individuals and private companies. They own the land, factories, and other resources needed to produce goods and services. In addition, economic choices are made privately. Workers are free to change jobs. People can spend their income any way they wish. Companies decide for themselves what to produce and how much to charge.

The first capitalist economy developed in Great Britain in the early 1800s, soon after the Industrial Revolution began. As Great Britain became an industrial country, it produced many more goods than before. This brought prosperity to many business owners.

At first, though, it did not bring prosperity to workers. They labored long hours for low wages. They lived crowded together in hastily built houses, without running water or sewer systems. Children as young as five years old worked in mines and factories from sunup to sundown.

Socialism

As a result of the workers' misery, some economists decided that the only solution was to get rid of capitalism. In its place, they proposed a different economic system called *socialism.*

Under socialism, the economy is controlled by the government. The government owns the land, factories, and other resources needed to produce

Capitalism in action (below left): President Roosevelt shakes hands with aircraft builder Howard Hughes. Norman Thomas (below right) ran for U.S. president as a socialist.

Karl Marx, the founder of Communism, wrote *The Communist Manifesto*.

goods and services. The government decides what to produce and how much to charge. Under socialism – so the theory goes – there are no rich and no poor. Everyone has a fair share of what is produced.

Most socialists believed that the best way to achieve socialism was through voting. So they organized workers' political parties. The Socialist party in the United States, for example, nominated Norman Thomas for president in 1932. He received almost 900,000 votes. Such nations as Great Britain, West Germany, Sweden, and Israel have had socialist governments at some time during the 20th century.

Communism

Some socialists, however, believed that it was not possible to achieve socialism through voting. The only way, they felt, was by violent revolution – overthrowing the government. The leading revolutionary socialist, or Communist, was a German philosopher named Karl Marx. His 1848 pamphlet *The Communist Manifesto*, co-written with Friedrich Engels, was a call to arms:

"Let the ruling classes tremble at a communist revolution. The proletarians [workers] have nothing to lose but their chains. They have a world to win.

"Workingmen of all countries, unite!"

In 1917, Communists took over the government of Russia in a revolution and established the Soviet Union. In 1949, Communists took over the government of China. ■

New Deal Q's and A's

Although the New Deal ended more than 50 years ago, many of its programs still affect people's lives. For example:

Q. You work in a supermarket. Does your employer have to pay you a certain amount per hour?

A. Yes. The Fair Labor Standards Act of 1938 set a minimum hourly wage for most workers. In those days, it was 40¢ an hour. The rate in 1991 was $4.25 an hour.

Q. You are 65 years old and have retired from your job. Are you entitled to a pension?

A. Yes. The Social Security Act of 1935 provides for old-age pensions. Both workers and their employers pay taxes for this. Under Medicare, adopted in 1965, Social Security also pays more than half the cost of hospital, nursing, and at-home care for older people.

Q. Your bank goes out of business. You had $10,000 in a savings account. Do you get your money back?

A. Yes. It is insured by the Federal Deposit Insurance Corporation (FDIC).

The War and the Economy

In 1940, the United States economy was still suffering from the effects of the Depression. The country was slowly getting better, but there were still problems. More than 14.6 percent of Americans were still out of work – about 8 million workers. The stock market was still weak. Industry grew slowly.

World War II made the United States and its economy snap to attention. The war effort put 12 million people to work in the armed forces. Millions more took jobs in the government and

A new aircraft carrier slides into the water in 1944. It was the 13th of its kind to be launched during the war.

industry. By 1944, only 1.2 million people were unemployed.

The money spent by the federal government on war made the expenses of the New Deal look like pocket change. In 1940, the cost of defense took up only 2.2 percent of the gross national product (GNP) – the total yearly value of the country's goods and services. By the time Pearl Harbor was bombed in December of 1941, military expenses were seven times greater – 16 percent of the GNP.

The Work of War

The United States had begun to prepare for war before the bombing of Pearl Harbor. In 1941, the Lend-Lease program began. With this program, the United States began lending, selling, or giving weapons and supplies to its allies. Between June of 1940 and December of 1945, the United States spent more than $261.5 billion on the war effort.

The United States' capitalist system was an important part of its war effort.

U.S. Troop and Plane Strength During World War II

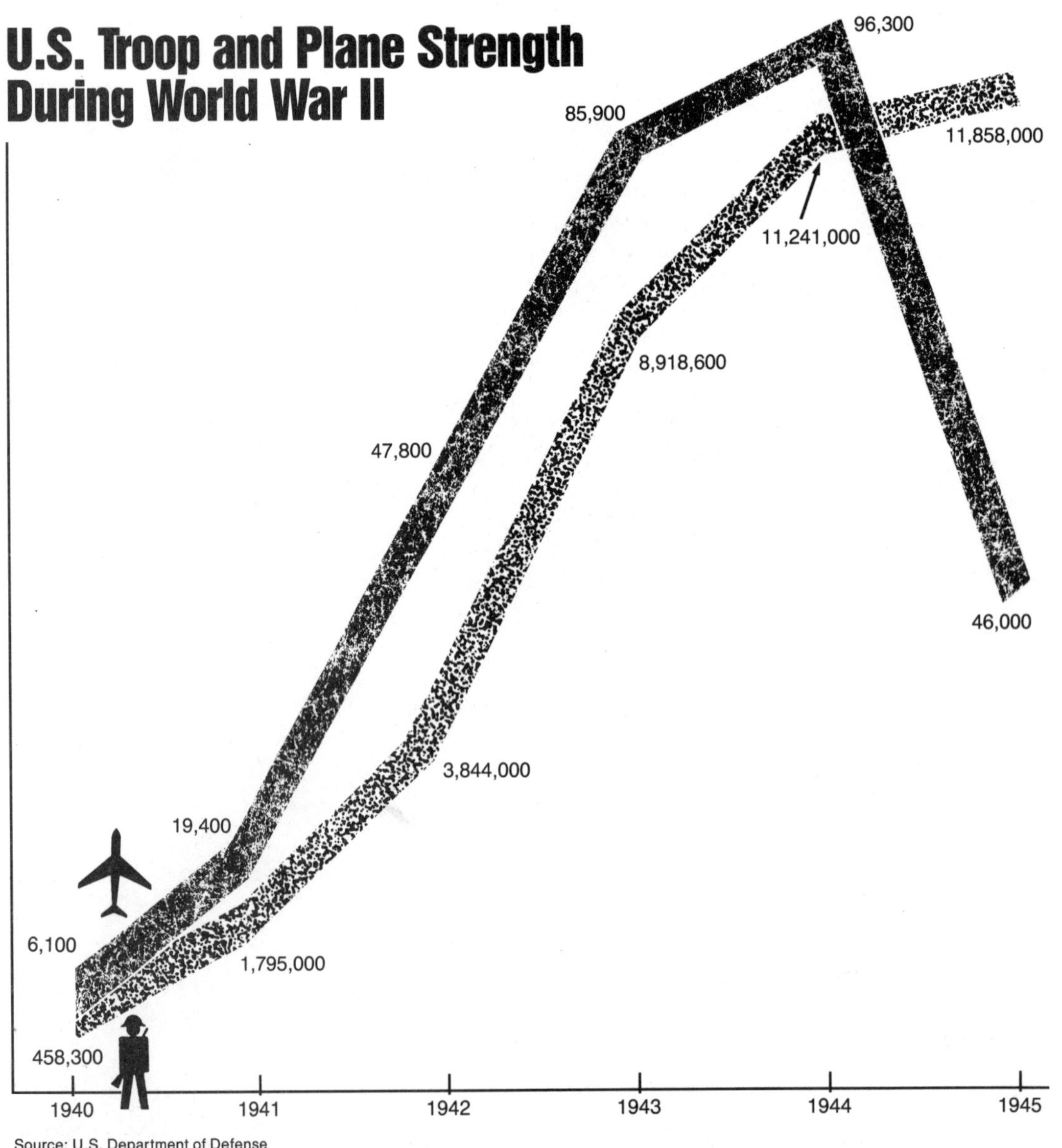

Source: U.S. Department of Defense

Big business and industry played an important role. War industries, such as shipyards, chemical factories, and aluminum factories, hired thousands of workers. Many had never held jobs in factories before, but they learned how to build what the war effort needed.

Big Business and Bonds

During the war, some smart small-business owners also became rich. They quickly got into high-profit industries. They became millionaires by dealing in scrap metal and canned goods.

But the government thought only large businesses could produce the huge number of items needed for war. Three-fourths of all military contracts went to 56 large companies. The government helped big business grow. Three-fourths of the money business needed to expand came from the government.

Taxes were raised very little during the war. But the government taxed more people than ever before – including poor people, who had never paid taxes. To come up with the billions of dollars it needed, the government borrowed money, printed more money, and "froze" prices and wages. And more than $200 billion was raised in war bonds bought by the American people.

Looking Ahead

Money alone did not win the war. Business spent the money well. It developed new manufacturing methods that helped the United States produce more than it ever had before. Increased production was one of the reasons the United States and its allies defeated the Axis powers.

And it also ended the Depression. After V-J (Victory in Japan) Day, the factories were still going strong. There was no going back to the days of high unemployment. No one would have chosen a war as the way out of the hard times. But at war's end, the U.S. economy was healthy again – and ready to grow even more. ■

The U.S. government thought that only big companies could produce things needed for World War II. Even today, some large companies are defense contractors. *They produce weapons that the government has agreed in advance to buy from them. Do you think this is a fair way of doing things? How could the government handle this differently?*

"If not for the war, the United States would never have gotten out of the Depression." People have said this over the years. Based on what you have read, do you think it is true? Why or why not?

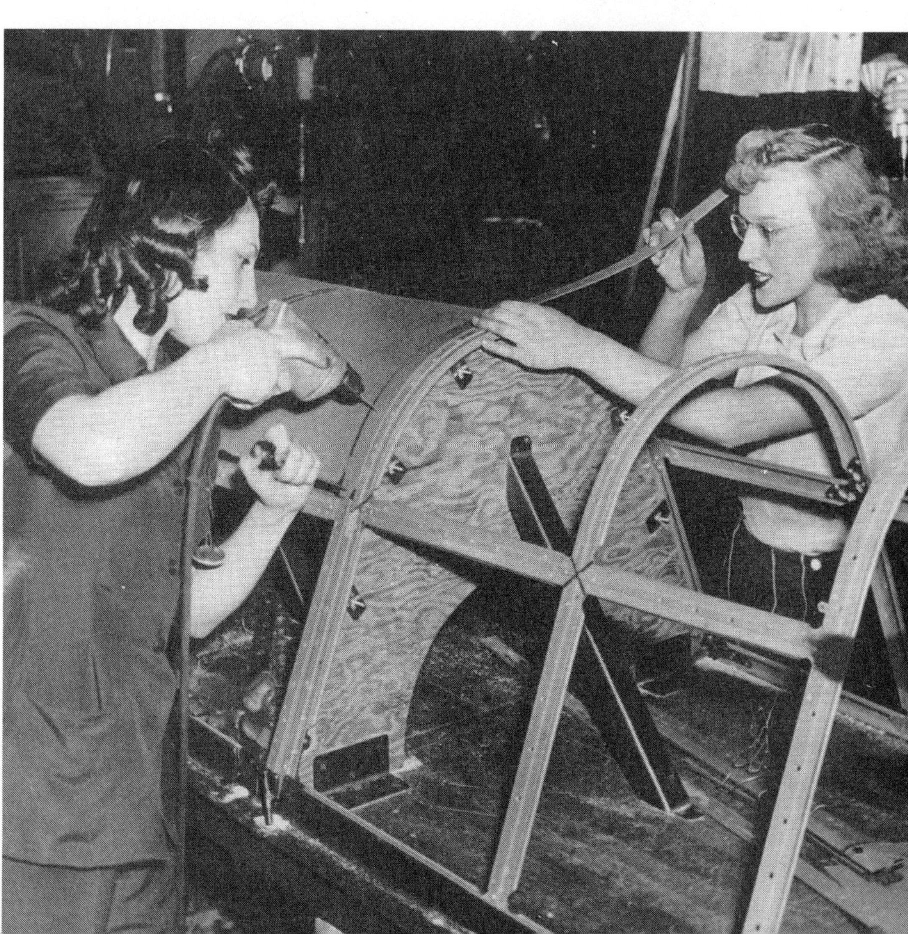

These factory workers are building an airplane cockpit.

The Scottsboro Case

It started in 1931 with a small incident – a fight on a freight train. By the time it ended 20 years later, the Scottsboro case was known all over the world. Millions of people had read about nine young blacks who had been falsely accused of raping two white women.

Found guilty and sentenced to death, the young men would have been executed if the case had not drawn such wide attention. The publicity given to the case put southern racism and injustice on display for the world to see.

Ruby Bates testifies in court in 1933. She admitted she had falsely accused nine black youths of rape.

Railroad to Prison

What really happened on that freight train? In March of 1931, the train, traveling through Alabama, bound for Memphis, Tennessee, carried some secret passengers. During the Depression, many people would "hobo" – hitch free rides on trains – as they looked for work. This train carried about 30 hoboes, most of them black. A fight erupted when some whites tried to push a black off the train. He and some other blacks reacted by throwing most of the whites off instead. These whites dusted themselves off and reported the fight to a stationmaster.

A deputy sheriff down the railroad line was told to "capture every Negro on the train and bring them to Scottsboro," the county seat. By the time he stopped the train, most of the fighters had gotten off. His men rounded up nine black youths, ages 12 to 19, and three whites.

Two of the whites were young women traveling together. After the blacks had been arrested, one of the women announced that she and her friend had been raped by the black youths.

Raping a white woman was the most serious crime a black could be accused of in the South. Some townspeople in Scottsboro, Alabama, wanted to skip the trial and go straight to the hanging. But the governor ordered that the blacks be protected, and they made it to court. Guards armed with bayonets and machine guns controlled the crowds that came to see the trial.

But problems lay ahead. The defense lawyers were unprepared, the youths' accusers were not telling the truth, and the jury was all white. Eight of the youths were quickly found guilty; the ninth was found guilty in a retrial. Spectators applauded each time a guilty verdict was announced. The youths were sentenced to death.

"Outsiders" Come In

The New York-based International Labor Defense (ILD) organization found out about the trial. The ILD had ties to the Communist party of the United States, which was trying to get the "oppressed masses" to join its ranks. The Scottsboro case was a great opportunity to recruit new members. Who was more oppressed than southern blacks?

The ILD and the Communist party did all they could to get the case in the news. Rallies, riots, and letters to newspapers made the Scottsboro case famous. Theodore Dreiser, a well-known American writer, called for new trials for the nine youths. Finally, the courts postponed their executions, and in 1932, they were granted new trials. But they couldn't find a new lawyer. Few lawyers wanted to be associated with the Communist party. New York criminal attorney Samuel Leibowitz finally agreed to defend the youths for free, on one condition: the Communists would have to tone down their speeches.

Although Leibowitz was a brilliant lawyer, he did not realize that the jury was deeply biased against blacks. He really thought the truth would set his first client, Haywood Patterson, free. It didn't. The jurors, all of them whites from the Scottsboro area, didn't like outsiders telling them how to think. They especially didn't like Jewish outsiders with Communist connections – like Leibowitz.

Leibowitz proved that one of the accusers, Victoria Price, was a prostitute and a liar. The second woman, Ruby Bates, admitted she had lied. Yet the jury once again found Patterson guilty and again sentenced him to death.

The Alabama National Guard had to be called to keep angry crowds from hanging the Scottsboro youths before their trial.

The Battle Goes On

So it went for several years and through a number of retrials. The case went all the way to the U.S. Supreme Court more than once. But Alabama's lieutenant governor was determined that the nine stay behind bars. Leibowitz was just as determined that they be freed.

Then, in 1937, it looked as though the Scottsboro nine might get a lucky break. The stubborn lieutenant governor had died, and his replacement was more reasonable. Suddenly, prosecutors dropped the charges against five of the nine, and four of them were then freed. (The fifth received a jail sentence for hitting an officer while trying to escape from jail.) It was never explained how five could be innocent and four guilty on the same evidence.

Of those still in jail, four were eventually paroled – the last one in 1950. The fifth man, Patterson, had escaped from prison in 1948 and fled to Michigan, where he went into hiding.

The Scottsboro case was a long, hard fight. But it produced two U.S. Supreme Court decisions that struck a blow for civil rights. One decision, in 1932, said that seven of the Scottsboro defendants had not been properly defended in their first trial. Another decision, in 1935, reversed the convictions of two defendants because there had been no blacks on the jury at their trial. From then on, minorities were more likely to get fairer trials with able lawyers and integrated juries, thanks to the Scottsboro youths. ■

Defense attorney Sam Leibowitz (above) with one of the accused youths. A sister of two of the accused youths (right) testifies.

CRIME BOSS

"Scarface" Al Capone was Chicago's most powerful crime boss.

"SEVEN CHICAGO GANGSTERS SLAIN BY FIRING SQUAD OF RIVALS," the headline of the *New York Times* read. "FACES TO WALL . . . THEY ARE MOWED DOWN."

Alphonse ("Al") Capone, also called "Scarface," was a hulking brute of a man. He had huge hands and a face scarred by a knife fight. Without pity, Capone murdered crime rivals. He wanted total control of organized crime in the Chicago area, and by the mid-1920s, he had it.

Capone was the man behind most of Chicago's alcohol, prostitution, and gambling operations. He also ran a "protection racket." This meant businesses paid him to let them operate unharmed. If they didn't pay, Capone destroyed them. "Protection" helped Capone become powerful.

Chicago's number-one crime boss was also one of the city's richest men. In 1927, he was said to be worth almost $100 million. Capone's success made him a hero to some local people. His expensive lifestyle was impressive at a time when so many people had so little. He "owned" politicians by bribing them, and he knew how to handle the press. He said he was not a criminal, but just a smart businessman. Many people believed him and looked up to this self-made man.

The St. Valentine's Day Massacre

By 1929, Capone ran all but the North Side of Chicago. George "Bugs" Moran controlled that part of town, and Capone wanted it. So on February 14, 1929, Scarface sent Bugs a valentine.

It happened at 10:30 A.M. on that sunny, very cold Valentine's Day. Moran's gang was relaxing in its headquarters – a garage. Suddenly, five men, three dressed as policemen, came in carrying submachine guns.

The police had made surprise visits before. But the five men were not real policemen. They were "hit men" – hired killers – working for Capone.

They made Moran's gang line up against the wall. Without warning, they opened fire on Moran's gang members. Seven of his top assistants were killed in the bloody attack.

There had been many gang-related killings in Chicago. But these killings, which the newspapers immediately called the "St. Valentine's Day Massacre," were the worst yet. The police had little doubt that Capone was behind the murders. Bugs Moran was sure. "Only Capone kills like that," he said. Capone was at the peak of his powers.

The brutal St. Valentine's Day Massacre made Al Capone a prime target of the federal government.

Yet the massacre also marked the beginning of Capone's fall from power. His brutal crime made national headlines. It also made him a national embarrassment. The newly elected president, Herbert Hoover, decided to get tough on Capone. His administration was determined to stop Capone any way it could.

Capone was smart; he didn't leave enough evidence to link him directly to the murders. But federal agents investigated his other crimes. The Justice Department targeted his alcohol operations. Agent Eliot Ness and his men found and smashed Capone's liquor-making "stills." This reduced his profits. Meanwhile, U.S. Treasury agents gathered proof that Capone had failed to pay taxes, and they took him to court. Finally, in 1931, "the feds"—government investigators—put him in jail for tax evasion.

Behind Bars at Last

Scarface couldn't buy his way out of trouble this time. He was tried and found guilty of tax evasion in October 1931. Capone was sentenced to 11 years in prison. He also was forced to pay $500,000 in back taxes and owed $80,000 in court costs and fines. His days as a crime boss were over. ■

Today, drug-dealing gangs are found in many cities. Their leaders are modern Al Capones. Judging from what you have read and heard:

What is the government doing to try to end drug crimes?

Do you think this effort will succeed? Why or why not?

Criminals like Al Capone became heroes in the eyes of many people. Today, in poor neighborhoods, young people often respect drug dealers and gang leaders. How do you explain this? What can be done about it?

The FBI Stays Busy

The 1930s were a decade of many big-time crooks – so many that the Federal Bureau of Investigation (FBI) needed help in catching them all. The FBI's "10 most wanted" list got the public involved. People could earn reward money for "fingering" criminals – that is, telling the FBI where to find them. This led to the fingering of John Dillinger.

The Daring Dillinger

Dillinger was the century's most famous bank robber at a time when many Americans hated banks. Some had lost their life savings to bank failures. Others had lost their homes or farms when they could not afford to pay back their bank loans. These people felt as if the banks had robbed them – so they were thrilled when Dillinger and his gang robbed the banks. And the Dillinger gang robbed plenty of them in the Midwest in 1933.

The real "brains" behind Dillinger's gang was the more experienced Harry Pierpont, but the police caught Pierpont early in 1934. Dillinger's gang began to split apart after that.

Dillinger disguised himself and headed for Chicago. His disguise didn't fool his girlfriend's roommate, Anna Sage. Sage fingered Dillinger and agreed to deliver him to the FBI.

Bad Night at the Biograph

Sage lured Dillinger to a movie theater, the Biograph, on the night of July 22, 1934. FBI agents surrounded the theater and waited for the movie to end. They watched for Anna Sage's bright red dress – and the man who would follow it.

When the movie ended, Dillinger left the theater with his girlfriend and Sage.

WANTED

JOHN HERBERT DILLINGER

On June 23, 1934, HOMER S. CUMMINGS, Attorney General of the United States, under the authority vested in him by an Act of Congress approved June 6, 1934, offered a reward of

$10,000.00

for the capture of John Herbert Dillinger or a reward of

$5,000.00

for information leading to the arrest of John Herbert Dillinger.

DESCRIPTION

Age, 32 years; Height, 5 feet 7-1/8 inches; Weight, 153 pounds; Build, medium; Hair, medium chestnut; Eyes, grey; Complexion, medium; Occupation, machinist; Marks and scars, 1/2 inch scar back left hand, scar middle upper lip, brown mole between eyebrows.

All claims to any of the aforesaid rewards and all questions and disputes that may arise as among claimants to the foregoing rewards shall be passed upon by the Attorney ... decisions shall be final and conclusive. The right is reserved to di... of said rewards as between several claimants. No ... official or employee of the Depart-

"Ma" Barker (above) and her husband in 1935. Clyde Barrow and Bonnie Parker (below) pose with their weapons.

Suddenly, they weren't beside him anymore. Dillinger sensed a trap and ran for an alley, but he didn't reach it. FBI agents shot him dead in seconds, ending his time as America's most spectacular crook.

More Desperate Characters

Bank robber "Baby Face" Nelson was a short man with a bad temper. The violent Nelson is best remembered for his own insane death.

Nelson's shoot-out with two FBI agents in November 1934 was a nightmare. Even after he was badly hurt, he kept shooting. He finally killed both men, then drove off. His body was found the next day – with 17 bullets in it.

Texans Bonnie Parker and Clyde Barrow became crime legends in the Southwest. They robbed, kidnapped, and killed – and they took photographs of themselves and sent them to the newspapers. Bonnie, who wrote poetry about crime, fascinated people. A tiny woman, she looked dwarfed by the huge guns she carried. But she knew how to use them, and with deadly accuracy.

"Pretty Boy" Floyd turned to crime in desperation after his farm failed. He then robbed banks in the Midwest and Southwest until the FBI stopped him.

The Barker family was perhaps the strangest gang of all. "Ma" Barker wanted her four boys to be outlaws. She got her wish. Teamed with robber Alvin Karpis and others, the "Bloody Barkers" kidnapped people and robbed banks, post offices, and payroll offices from Minnesota to Texas. It was difficult for the FBI to capture them, because it was so tough to predict how and where the Barkers would strike next. One by one, however, the Barkers were caught or killed.

Before the end of the 1930s, most of the major criminals of the decade were either dead or in jail. The United States was becoming a safer place, and the era of the big-time crook was ending. ■

Mug shots of Charles "Pretty Boy" Floyd. Floyd was said to have robbed more than thirty midwestern banks.

The Violent Thirties

Newspaper stories about the major crimes of the 1930s paint a picture of bank robberies, bloody fights among organized crime members, kidnappings, and dramatic trials. Why were there so many crimes during the decade?

Some of the reasons go back to the 1920s. Criminals took advantage of the government's "hands-off" attitude toward business during that era. It was a decade of illegal deals and mergers and stock scams. Prohibition also added to the lawlessness of the 1920s. Many people who usually obeyed the law broke the law banning the sale of alcohol. They flocked to secret bars, or speakeasies, to buy illegal drinks. While there, some took part in other forms of illegal fun, such as gambling. Organized crime grew in major American cities by supplying liquor to speakeasies.

Then, near the end of the 1920s, the stock market collapsed. So did the economy. Suddenly, millions of Americans were thrown out of their jobs and homes. Roads and railways were filled with these homeless people, all of them looking for jobs that no longer existed. Many Americans lost hope and grew desperate.

Desperate people do desperate things. Some people turned to crime in this era because they felt they had nothing more to lose. Some bank robbers of the 1930s had been raised in poverty and had little respect for other people's property. Others simply took advantage of a time when police driving old cars couldn't keep up with criminals' fast getaway cars. Police couldn't chase crooks across state lines anyway.

National Tragedy

The kidnapper's ladder (right) rests against the bedroom window of Charles Lindbergh, Jr. Below, headlines announce the crime.

"Extra! Extra! Read all about it," newsboys shouted. "LINDBERGH BABY KIDNAPPED FROM HOME OF PARENTS . . . TAKEN FROM HIS CRIB; WIDE SEARCH ON," the headlines read. "MOTHER CARRIES ON WITH BRAVE SMILE, BUT DRAWN FACE AND TREMBLE OF LIPS BETRAY ANGUISH AS SHE WAITS FOR NEWS," they added later.

It was one of the hottest news stories of the 1930s. On March 1, 1932, someone had climbed a homemade ladder to an upstairs nursery and stolen the most famous baby in America. "The chubby, golden-haired boy closely resembling his famous father" was the only child of pilot Charles A. Lindbergh.

In 1927, Charles Lindbergh had become the first to fly nonstop from New York to Paris. Almost overnight, the boyishly handsome man had become a popular hero. Since then, he had grown even more popular. His

W YORK, WEDNESDAY, MARCH 2, 1932.

on Dry Law Test;
lls Up in Wheelchair

LINDBERGH BABY KIDNAPPED FROM HOME
OF PARENTS ON FARM NEAR PRINCETON;
TAKEN FROM HIS CRIB; WIDE SEARCH O

CHILD STOLEN IN EVE

NEW YORK, FRIDAY, MAY 13, 1932.

t Relief Plan
to Use as Loans

Proposal Before Colleagues—
p States Handle Jobless

LINDBERGH BABY FOUND DEAD NEAR HOME;
MURDERED SOON AFTER THE KIDNAPPING
72 DAYS AGO AND LEFT LYING IN WOOD

BODY MILE FROM HOPEW

PPERS LEFT SLAIN BABY.

WANTED
INFORMATION AS TO THE WHEREABOUTS OF
CHAS. A. LINDBERGH, JR.
OF HOPEWELL, N. J.
SON OF COL. CHAS. A. LINDBERGH
World-Famous Aviator
This child was kidnaped from his home in Hopewell, N. J., between 8 and 10 p.m. on Tuesday, March 1, 1932.
DESCRIPTION:
Age, 20 months — Hair, blond, curly
Weight, 27 to 30 lbs. — Eyes, dark blue
Height, 29 inches — Complexion, light
Deep dimple in center of chin
Dressed in one-piece coverall night suit
ADDRESS ALL COMMUNICATIONS TO
COL. H. N. SCHWARZKOPF, TRENTON, N. J., or
COL. CHAS. A. LINDBERGH, HOPEWELL, N. J.
ALL COMMUNICATIONS WILL BE TREATED IN CONFIDENCE
March 11, 1932
COL. H. NORMAN SCHWARZKOPF
Supt. New Jersey State Police, Trenton, N. J.

A reward poster (above left) of the New Jersey state police. A grim-faced Charles Lindbergh (above right) arrives at the courthouse.

marriage and, later, the birth of his son had received a lot of publicity – too much for the pilot's liking. So he had a home built in the New Jersey countryside, far away from the public eye. The Lindberghs had barely moved in when the kidnapper struck and shattered their dreams. Horrified Americans considered this kidnapping to be a national tragedy.

The Tragedy Deepens

The kidnapper demanded a $50,000 ransom, and the Lindberghs paid it. Included in the money were some "marked" bills from the Treasury Department. The Lindberghs were then told where they could find their 20-month-old son. But the child was not there. Around the world, searches for the baby continued.

Then, in May of 1932, came the bad news: "LINDBERGH BABY FOUND DEAD NEAR HOME; MURDERED SOON AFTER THE KIDNAPPING 72 DAYS AGO AND LEFT LYING IN THE WOODS." The man who found the body spoke for many when he said: "I just hope they get the man that did it. Nothing would be too bad to do to him."

Catching the Kidnapper

The hunt for the kidnapper grew more intense. Yet police had few clues. They did have reason to believe that the kidnapper had been born in Germany, but that wasn't much help. The area where the kidnapping took place was full of German immigrants.

A break in the case came late in 1934. Some of the "marked" ransom money appeared in New York. Police traced it to a German-born carpenter named Bruno Richard Hauptmann. They arrested him.

Hauptmann had nearly $15,000 of the ransom money hidden in his garage. He said the money came from a business partner who owed him money.

Few believed his story. His partner was dead, so he could not prove it was true. Also, Hauptmann had a criminal record for theft back in Germany.

Then a wood expert examined the ladder left behind by the kidnapper. He declared that its boards came from Hauptmann's attic.

Hauptmann on trial. He was found guilty in 1935 and was executed in 1936.

Hauptmann's Trial

Americans had waited almost three years for this moment. News coverage of the six-week-long trial pushed everything else into the background. The trial was in Flemington, New Jersey, and 700 reporters crammed into the small town. Its tiny courthouse couldn't hold all the people fighting to get inside. Those who did get in had to pay for their seats.

Writer Edna Ferber said that the crowd's lust for blood made her "want to resign from the human race." Souvenir sellers sold tiny models of the kidnapper's ladder. Writer Damon Runyon reported that bets were being placed on the trial's outcome. These incidents helped make it a sad time for American justice.

In February 1935, Hauptmann was found guilty and was sentenced to die in the electric chair. Though he continued to swear he was innocent, he was executed in 1936.

The "Lindbergh Laws"

This case heightened Americans' concern about kidnapping. It was estimated that 2,000 kidnappings had occurred between 1930 and 1932. The Lindbergh case sped the passage of several antikidnapping laws already in the works. Called the "Lindbergh Laws," they made kidnapping a federal offense punishable by death. ■

THEN & NOW

The Lindbergh case isn't over for Hauptmann's widow, Anna. She is still convinced her husband was innocent. In 1983, she sued New Jersey for executing her husband. Her suit failed, but not her determination. In 1990, at age 91, Anna Hauptmann was still trying to get New Jersey's governor to clear her husband's name.

National Shame

"Being at Rowher was just a lonely feeling that I can't explain," Miyo Senzaki recalls. "You couldn't run anywhere. It was scary because there was no end to it. You could run and run . . . but where are you to go? It was just nothing but water and then there were rattlesnakes. We felt like prisoners."

Senzaki, describing one of 10 concentration camps in America during World War II, wasn't alone in that feeling. Although the concentration camps were sometimes called by nicer names, such as "relocation" or "internment" camps, they were actually prisons. And nearly 110,000 Japanese-American men, women, and children were forced to live in them. Wartime fears and old hatreds were responsible for putting them there. Japan's bombing of Pearl Harbor on December 7, 1941, shocked Americans deeply and convinced many that all Japanese were dangerous.

The Mochida family, like other West Coast Japanese-Americans, was sent to a camp.

Unpopular Immigrants

But distrust of the Japanese didn't begin with Pearl Harbor. It began soon after Japanese immigrants first arrived in the United States in the 1880s.

The first Japanese immigrants had been brought to Hawaii, then a U.S. territory, by pineapple plantation owners who needed workers. The Japanese settled in Hawaii in great numbers. A smaller number of these farmers headed for the U.S. mainland and landed on the West Coast. Many stayed in California.

At first, California's major fruit and vegetable growers welcomed these newcomers. The Japanese were reliable, hard workers who worked for less money than native migrant workers.

But it was only temporary work, and the Japanese wanted more security. After a few seasons of working for others, many had saved enough to buy their own small pieces of land so that they could grow their own crops.

The growers, however, didn't want to lose their best source of labor. They wanted a law that would keep Japanese immigrants from buying land. To get lawmakers' support, the growers spread fears about the Japanese. They warned that these "foreigners" would buy up all the good land and drive native farmers out of business.

No Japanese Wanted!

The growers got their way. The Alien Land Bill, which kept noncitizens from buying land, was passed. Since Japanese immigrants were not allowed to be citizens, the law kept them from owning their own farms. Their American-born children could buy land, but not until they were adults.

The growers' lies had taken root. Many people would have nothing to do with the Japanese and tried to keep them out of clubs and businesses. West Coast natives let their politicians know that they wanted their Japanese neighbors to leave.

Then Pearl Harbor fueled the anti-Japanese feeling. People feared that Japanese-Americans were spies for Tokyo. There was talk about a Japanese spy ring operating in Los Angeles in the spring of 1941.

Rumors flew that Japan's navy planned to attack the West Coast with the help of local spies. Newspapers and powerful politicians spread these fears. California attorney general Earl Warren said that anyone who trusted Japanese-Americans was "living in a fool's paradise."

By April 1942, the government was arresting Japanese-Americans . . . . They could bring with them only what they could carry. Most lost their homes, businesses, crops, and savings.

Memories of Damaged Lives

Some losses can't be mended. Donald Nakahata's father was moved from camp to camp for questioning, and Nakahata never saw him again. "It's . . . sad . . . that I don't know where he died," Nakahata says.

Tom Watanabe's wife gave birth to twin girls in the Manzanar camp. There were complications afterward, and his wife and babies died. "I know for a fact . . . that the camp did not have the facilities [to handle medical emergencies]," Watanabe remembers. All the camp hospitals were little more than sheds. They were understaffed and badly equipped. Registered nurse Emi Somekawa says "there were a lot of unnecessary deaths in camp" because of such conditions.

The camps broke the spirit of some of their older inmates. On release, Akana Imamura said, "We are encouraged to relocate again into the world as a stranger in strange communities. . . . Where shall we go?"

A Bad Order

Finally, President Franklin D. Roosevelt bowed to public pressure. On February 19, 1942, he signed Executive Order 9066. It allowed the U.S. Army to make the West Coast a "military zone" and to place Japanese-Americans in camps.

By April 1942, the government was arresting Japanese-Americans. They were forced to move into "assembly centers" until the camps were completed. They could bring with them only what they could carry. Most lost their homes, businesses, crops, and savings.

Their first new homes were often drafty, smelly horse barns. Later, they were moved into quickly built concentration camps fenced in with barbed wire. They lived in barracks (large, temporary buildings) that had gaps in the walls and floors. The barracks did not keep out the heat or cold, and the camps were troubled by dust storms, bad water, and harsh weather. Many people shared single-room dwellings, and sickness spread easily.

The prisoners had no privacy. Armed

THEN & NOW

It's 50 years overdue, but Japanese-Americans are getting their apology. After decades of talk about trying to make up for the tragedy, the U.S. Congress passed a reparation bill in 1988. It permits a payment of $20,000 to each camp internee still living.

In 1990, attorney general Dick Thornburgh handed out the first of these checks and presidential apologies to nine elderly people. It was a start, but the government still had 65,000 survivors to reach.

guards in towers watched everyone's movements. Families were separated. Parents found it hard to control their children. Many newborn babies got their first look at America in these places. For older Japanese who died there, it was a bitter last taste of America.

By late 1943, the government was beginning to realize its mistake. Young Japanese-American men from the camps had joined the armed services and proved their patriotism in battle. General Douglas MacArthur said that the Japanese-American soldiers "saved a million lives and shortened the war by two years" with their brave fighting. But public fear of the Japanese continued. It would be another year before President Roosevelt would order the camps to start closing down.

After their release, the Japanese-Americans faced another problem. It would take years for them to rebuild their lives. Some would never again feel safe in the "land of the free." ■

During World War II, many Americans believed that Japanese-Americans wanted to hurt the United States.

Talk with people who lived through the war years. What do they think about the imprisonment of Japanese-Americans? If they knew about it at the time, what did they think then? What did they think about the Japanese in general at the time?

To understand more about the treatment of Japanese-Americans during the war years, read Farewell to Manzanar, *by Jeanne Wakatsuki Houston. She is a Japanese-American who was imprisoned with her family during that time.*

Although anti-German feelings also existed during the war, German-Americans were not imprisoned as the West Coast Japanese-Americans were. Why do you think they were not?

Japanese–Americans line up for inspection outside their tents in 1942.

A Time of Building

President Hoover was on hand to turn a key that lit up New York City's Empire State Building at its official opening on May 1, 1931. New York's popular former governor, Al Smith, looked on with pride as his grandchildren cut the ribbon to officially open the building. The building was, said Smith, the world's greatest monument to human skill, mind, and muscle. In just over eight months, its 102-story steel skeleton had risen above Manhattan at a speed that surprised even the workers who were building it.

The Chrysler Building (left) and the Empire State Building (right), two famous New York City skyscrapers built in the 1930s.

The Sky's the Limit

Just as the automobile helped cities spread *out*, the skyscraper helped cities grow *up*. The first skyscrapers were built in the late 1800s. By the 1930s, they were changing the look of America's big cities. In New York City, the race was on to build the world's tallest skyscraper.

In 1929, builders had completed the Manhattan Building – at 927 feet, the world's tallest office building, though not for long. Only a few months later, the 1,046-foot Chrysler Building set a new record. Then, in 1931, the Empire State Building took the title. At 1,250 feet, the Empire State towered over Manhattan as the world's tallest building for more than 40 years.

Not everyone was thrilled with the skyscraper boom, however. Some city officials and residents worried that skyscrapers would create dark, dangerous "canyons." They were afraid that skyscrapers would block the sunlight and change gentle winds into howling gales when they were squeezed between the tall buildings. As early as 1908, people were warned that "the so-called 'skyscraper' [is] a menace to public health and safety."

The architects of the skyscrapers listened to their critics and came up with daring new designs. Instead of the huge, boxlike buildings that had been built earlier, many skyscrapers of the 1930s were built like graceful spires that grew narrower toward the top. Architects also surrounded skyscrapers with smaller, lower buildings and open space. This new approach to design can still be seen, for example, in Rockefeller Center in New York City. It proved to the skyscrapers' critics that tall could be beautiful – and safe.

Bridges to the Future

As the skyscrapers reached new heights, bridges built in the 1930s reached new lengths. These new bridges, together with the automobile and the fast-growing highway system, cut travel time to the nation's cities.

In 1931, New York's 3,500-foot George Washington Bridge, which spans the Hudson River to connect New York City to New Jersey, broke the record for the world's longest bridge. But only six years later, in 1937, the Golden Gate Bridge in San Francisco set a new record. The single span of the Golden Gate, suspended between two huge towers, stretches 4,200 feet across the entrance to San Francisco Bay. In 1964, New York's Verrazano-Narrows set a new record by 60 feet.

The great skyscrapers and bridges of the 1930s set new records for height and distance. And their designs affected the look of America's cities for years to come. ■

San Francisco's Golden Gate Bridge was the longest bridge in the world for almost three decades.

Why are people so impressed by tall buildings? How do they make people feel? Write a paragraph about a time when you looked up at a skyscraper – or down at the ground from the top floor.

Aviation Triumph and Tragedy

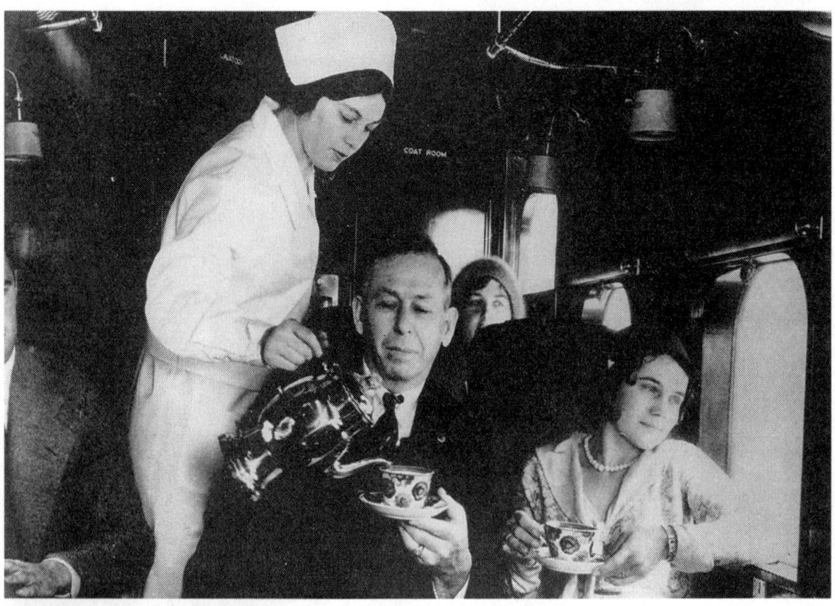

Air travel was a new luxury (top) in the 1930s. Amelia Earhart (bottom) was the first woman to receive the Distinguished Flying Cross award.

"Here I am," said a handsome air traveler in a 1930s magazine ad, "the fellow who said he would never fly! If I'd thought it was anything like this, I'd have been flying long ago! Here I am, enjoying undreamed-of travel comforts, seeing beauty I never knew existed, saving days of time!"

Discoverers of a new world: that is how the airline industry described passengers on the world's newest form of transportation. "You, too," the ad told Americans, "have only to try it to know that the sooner you adopt it, the sooner you catch up with other modern folks!"

Throughout the 1930s, Americans were caught up in a fever that the press called "air mindedness." Millions of Americans listened to popular radio programs about flying. Airplane races drew large crowds. At the same time, airplanes were becoming faster and safer. As a result, the young airline industry began regular passenger service between the United States, South America, and Asia using aircraft like the *China Clipper.*

But tragedy was never far away. Many famous pilots lost their lives blazing new trails through the air. For the first time, passengers also lost their lives in air disasters.

Amelia Earhart, Queen of the Air

No one represented the triumph and the tragedy of flying better than Amelia Earhart. She was the first woman to fly alone across the Atlantic Ocean from the United States to Europe. As a result, she was nicknamed "Lady Lindy" after Charles Lindbergh, the first man to fly solo to Europe. Earhart set records, made long-distance tours, and flew in races. She made a solo flight from Hawaii to California in 1935. And she was the first woman to receive the Distinguished Flying Cross, a medal awarded by the U.S. government for flying achievement.

But in 1937 tragedy struck. Earhart and her navigator, Fred Noonan, had set out to make an around-the-world trip. They had finished nearly two-thirds of the flight when they mysteriously disappeared in the central Pacific Ocean. They were never found, and to this day, no one is sure what happened during their flight.

Disaster at Lakehurst

Earhart and Noonan disappeared less than two months after another air disaster had shocked America. On May 6, 1937, the German blimp *Hindenburg* (a lighter-than-air craft filled with hydrogen) burst into flames over Lakehurst, New Jersey.

Herb Morrison was covering the *Hindenburg* story for radio station WLS in Chicago. His report:

> Here it comes, ladies and gentlemen, and what a sight it is, a thrilling one, a marvelous sight. . . . The sun is striking the windows of the observation deck on the westward side and sparkling like glittering jewels on the background of black velvet. . . . Oh, oh, oh! It's burst into flames. . . . Get out of the way, please, oh my, this is terrible, oh my, get out of the way please! It is burning, bursting into flames, and is falling . . . Oh! This is one of the worst . . . Oh! . . . and all the humanity! . . .

The next day, papers around the world printed terrifying photos of the scene. Partly because of the *Hindenburg* disaster, travel by blimp never caught on. But today, safer helium-filled blimps help television show baseball and football games. ■

What do you think might have happened to Amelia Earhart? Write a short story about the last hours of her life—as they might have been.

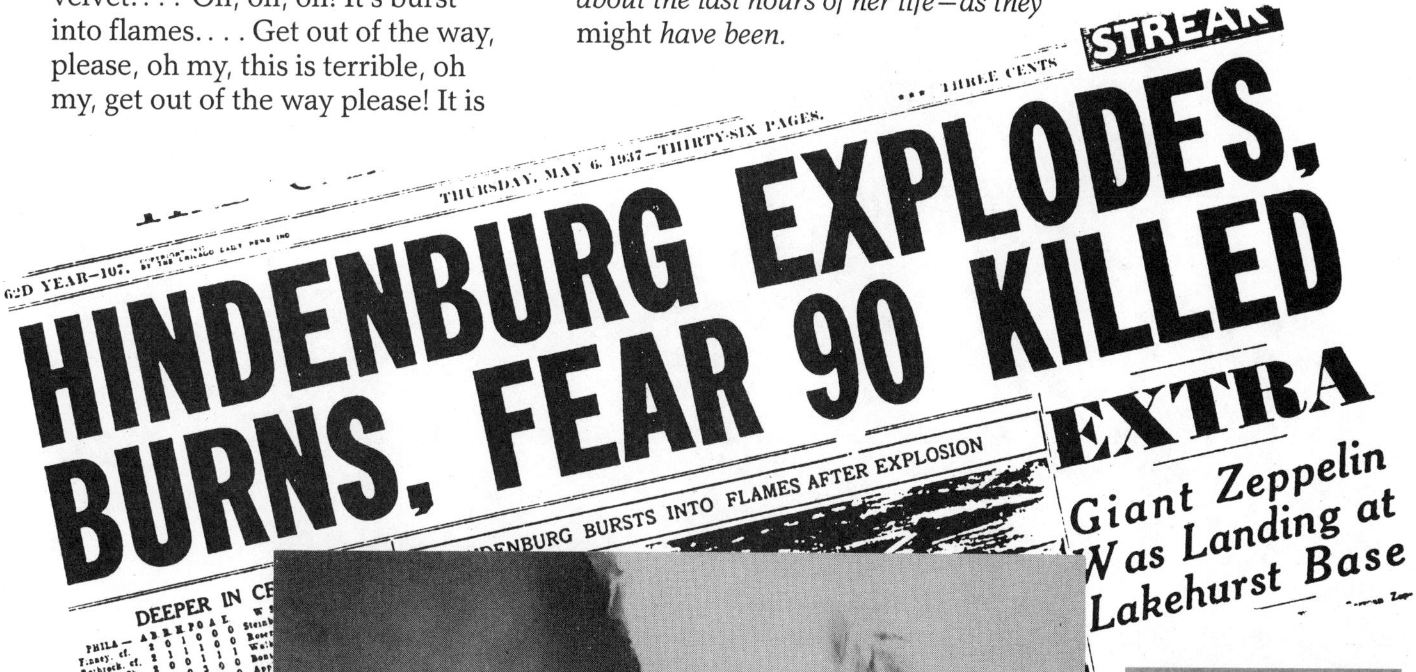
STREAK
THREE CENTS
THURSDAY, MAY 6, 1937—THIRTY-SIX PAGES.
62D YEAR—107.
HINDENBURG EXPLODES, BURNS, FEAR 90 KILLED
EXTRA
HINDENBURG BURSTS INTO FLAMES AFTER EXPLOSION
Giant Zeppelin Was Landing at Lakehurst Base
DEEPER IN CE

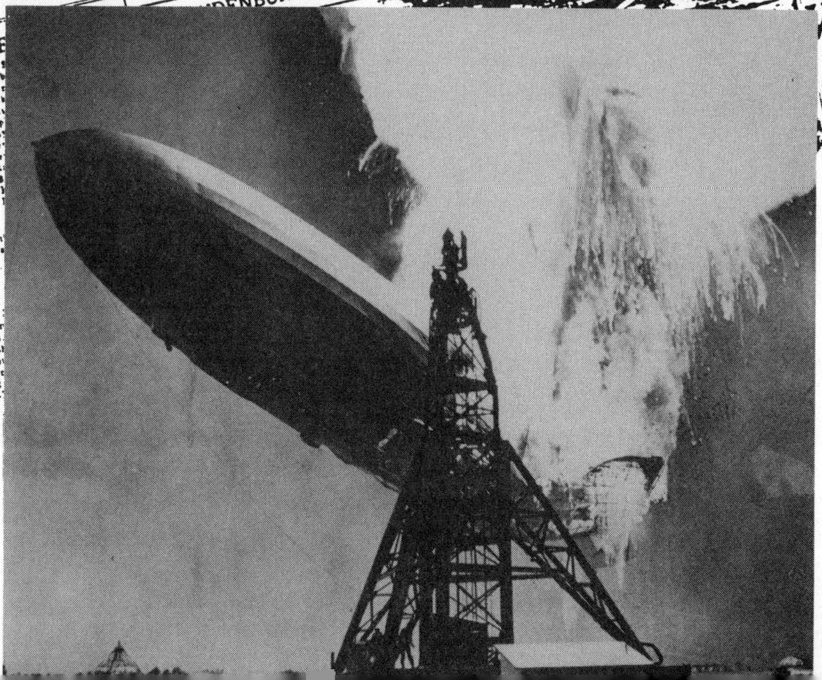

The giant airship *Hindenburg* explodes.

Power to the People—the TVA

The Tennessee River snakes its way for 652 miles through the heart of the American South. Before 1933, it was hard to use this big river to travel and make electricity, because the level of water changed as seasons changed. This problem kept companies from building factories in the river valley. What's more, the valley's farmland was poor and getting worse because of soil erosion (loss of the rich topsoil needed for growing). With little industry or farming, the Tennessee Valley was one of the nation's poorest regions.

To attack these problems, Senator George Norris of Nebraska urged President Roosevelt to create the

Tennessee Valley Authority, or TVA. Roosevelt agreed, and in 1933 he set up the TVA to control all federal agencies in the Tennessee Valley. For the first time, the U.S. government would manage the natural and economic resources of an entire region.

At the heart of the TVA was a bold plan. A set of dams controlled the river's flow. Engineers deepened and widened the river channel and added locks to make it easier for riverboat pilots to steer their way through the winding river. At the same time, the dams generated cheap electricity for industry and the people living in the valley. In addition, the TVA set up soil conservation programs to restore damaged land and improve farming. It also began programs to kill mosquitoes that spread malaria, a common disease in the valley.

Fierce Fights

The TVA had many enemies. Local power companies and other businesses fought hard against it. They objected to what they saw as unfair competition from the federal government. The power companies took the TVA to court. But in 1936, the U.S. Supreme Court decided that the TVA was legal.

By the 1960s, the TVA had met many of its goals. Its 48 dams and other plants created the largest single electric power system in the world. The lakes created by the dams also helped the area make money by attracting vacationers. River traffic, commerce, farming, and the annual income of the valley's residents all increased. The government was in the business of controlling the environment. ■

The TVA was the first time the government got involved in making electric power—and in controlling the environment. Do you think the government should be involved in these kinds of projects? Why or why not?

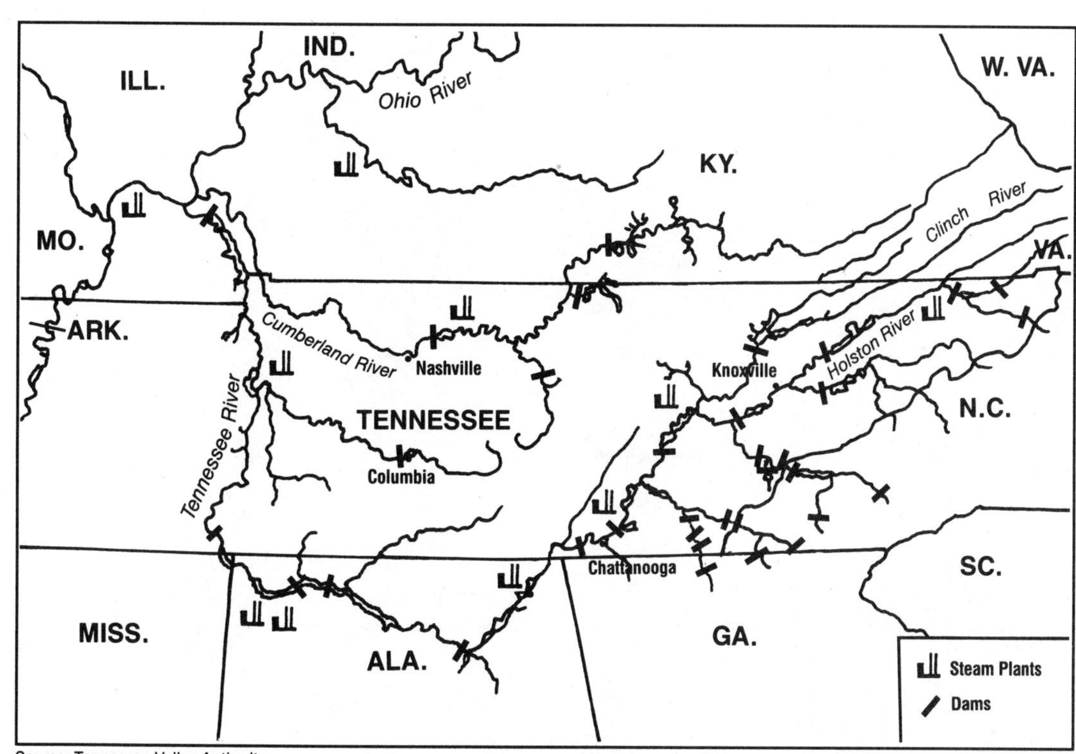

Source: Tennessee Valley Authority

A scene of poverty (far left) near Wadesboro, North Carolina, in 1938. A map (left) of the Tennessee Valley Authority.

The Manhattan Project

Hungarian physicist Leo Szilard had an idea while he waited to cross a busy London street one day in 1933. As the light changed from green to red, Szilard realized something. With the right chemical element and under the right conditions, scientists could split atoms in a chain reaction that would give off great energy. This idea formed the basis for the atomic bomb.

By 1939, Nazi Germany was working hard to create an atomic weapon. Szilard and other scientists who had fled the Nazis urged Albert Einstein,

The Manhattan Project developed the first nuclear bomb. Here, project director J. Robert Oppenheimer (left) inspects the site of the first test explosion.

the most famous scientist of the day, to write to President Roosevelt. In his now-famous letter of August 2, 1939, Einstein alerted the president that "extremely powerful bombs of a new type" could be constructed. He warned that Germany was involved in nuclear research and had the raw material necessary for creating a nuclear chain reaction. Einstein also told Roosevelt that atomic research by the United States was very important. Roosevelt agreed with Einstein. The president moved quickly to have U.S. scientists work to develop an atomic weapon.

After the United States entered World War II, the atomic weapon project became a huge, nationwide effort. The headquarters was in the area of New York City known as Manhattan, so the effort to create the atom bomb was called the Manhattan Project.

A National Effort

In a way, the Manhattan Project was strange: it involved the work of thousands of people – but it was a secret. Important work on the project was done at locations across the United States. In Berkeley, California, and the newly created city of Oak Ridge, Tennessee, scientists worked to find the chemical elements needed for the bomb. At the University of Chicago, under the football stadium, Enrico Fermi achieved a sustained nuclear chain reaction on December 2, 1942. Szilard's idea was now reality.

The first atomic bomb was built in the desert of New Mexico at Los Alamos, a town built for the project. Hundreds of top engineers and scientists lived and worked there from 1943 to 1945. Their director, J. Robert Oppenheimer, said, ". . . almost everyone knew that his job, if

Debate over A-Bomb Use

"This [the atomic bomb] is the Second Coming, in wrath."
Winston Churchill, July 1945

In July of 1945, the Allies had called for Japan to surrender and end World War II. They had warned Japan that it would face destruction if it did not stop fighting. But the Japanese had ignored the demand. So Harry Truman, who had been president for only three months, faced a very difficult decision: invade Japan or drop the atomic bomb.

As Truman thought about his decision, the U.S. Army prepared to invade the Japanese homeland. Experts told Truman that the invasion would cost the United States 500,000 dead and wounded. Japanese military and civilian casualties would be even greater. Japan would probably be destroyed in the process. So Truman decided that dropping the atomic bomb would end the war quickly with less loss of life. In the end, the blasts of Hiroshima and Nagasaki killed more than 200,000 Japanese.

Many disagreed with Truman's use of the bomb. Leo Szilard wrote to President Truman a few days after Hiroshima and Nagasaki. He called using the bomb "a flagrant violation of our moral standards." Even today, debate continues over Truman's decision. But few would argue that it was an easy choice.

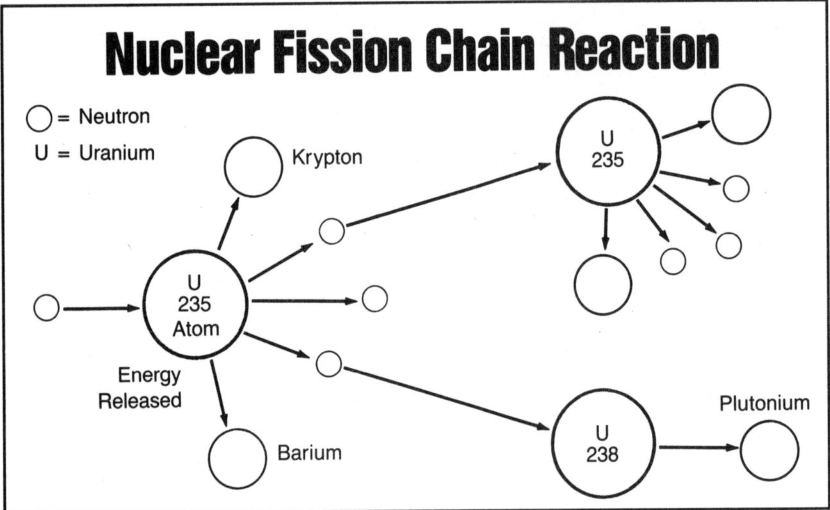

This diagram shows how nuclear fission works. Splitting the atom starts a chain reaction.

achieved, would be a part of history."

Two types of atomic bombs were made at Los Alamos. One used the element uranium to fuel the atomic reaction. The other used plutonium. Both were elements with atoms that could split in a chain reaction. On July 16, 1945, the plutonium atomic bomb was exploded successfully in the New Mexico desert. The atomic age had begun.

Day of Destruction

On August 6, 1945, the United States used atomic weapons for the first time. The U.S. bomber plane *Enola Gay* dropped a uranium atomic bomb, nicknamed "Little Boy," on Hiroshima, Japan.

The atomic bomb offered a chance to end the war quickly. Although Germany had already surrendered, Japan fought on. The United States hoped that the bombing would help the Allies avoid a long and bloody invasion of Japan.

The bomb exploded with the force of 20,000 tons of dynamite. In an instant, much of the city was destroyed. "Ah, that instant! I felt as though I had been struck by a hammer and thrown in boiling oil," wrote a young survivor. A

THEN & NOW

After the destruction of Hiroshima, scientists tried to find peaceful uses for atomic power. One use was generating electricity. If a nuclear reaction could be closely controlled, the heat created would make steam to power electrical generators. Engineers hoped that nuclear reactions might someday replace all other energy sources.

But people became concerned about the safety of nuclear power. What if a nuclear reaction went out of control and caused an explosion? What about the materials left over from a controlled reaction? They are highly radioactive and deadly – and stay that way for hundreds of years. How could this deadly waste be safely disposed of? These questions and others have caused many countries to stop using nuclear power.

In the United States today, the use of nuclear power to make electricity is hotly debated. Some say nuclear power is the cheapest and safest way to provide energy. Others say that all nuclear power plants should be closed because of the possibility of a disaster. Questions about the long-term safety of the peaceful use of atomic energy remain.

doctor said the explosion was like "the collapse of the earth."

The Japanese did not ask for peace after Hiroshima. So a larger, more powerful plutonium atomic bomb was dropped on Nagasaki on August 9. This bomb, called "Fat Man," had the force of 22,000 tons of dynamite.

Japan's Emperor Hirohito asked for peace a few days after the Nagasaki bombing, saying that Japan could not continue to fight against "a new and most cruel bomb." World War II was over. But the success of the Manhattan Project had set the demon of atomic warfare loose in the world. ■

What is your opinion about the bombing of Hiroshima and Nagasaki? Do you believe that it was the quickest way to end the war, with the fewest people dying? Or, like Leo Szilard, do you think it was wrong to use atom bombs?

Do you think it could be right for any country to use nuclear weapons again?

Do you think any country ever will?

The *Enola Gay* (above) dropped "Little Boy" (below) on Hiroshima. The bomb exploded with the force of 20,000 tons of TNT.

Medical Advances

In 1935, a badly bleeding patient at a London hospital was given a treatment that would make medical history. Two doctors had found a way to replace the patient's lost blood with blood dripped from a bottle through a rubber tube and into a needle in the patient's arm. They could carefully control the flow with a clamp on the tube.

Blood transfusions – replacing blood lost in bleeding – had been done before, but the procedure had always been very risky. In the early 1900s, the blood vessel of a person donating the blood

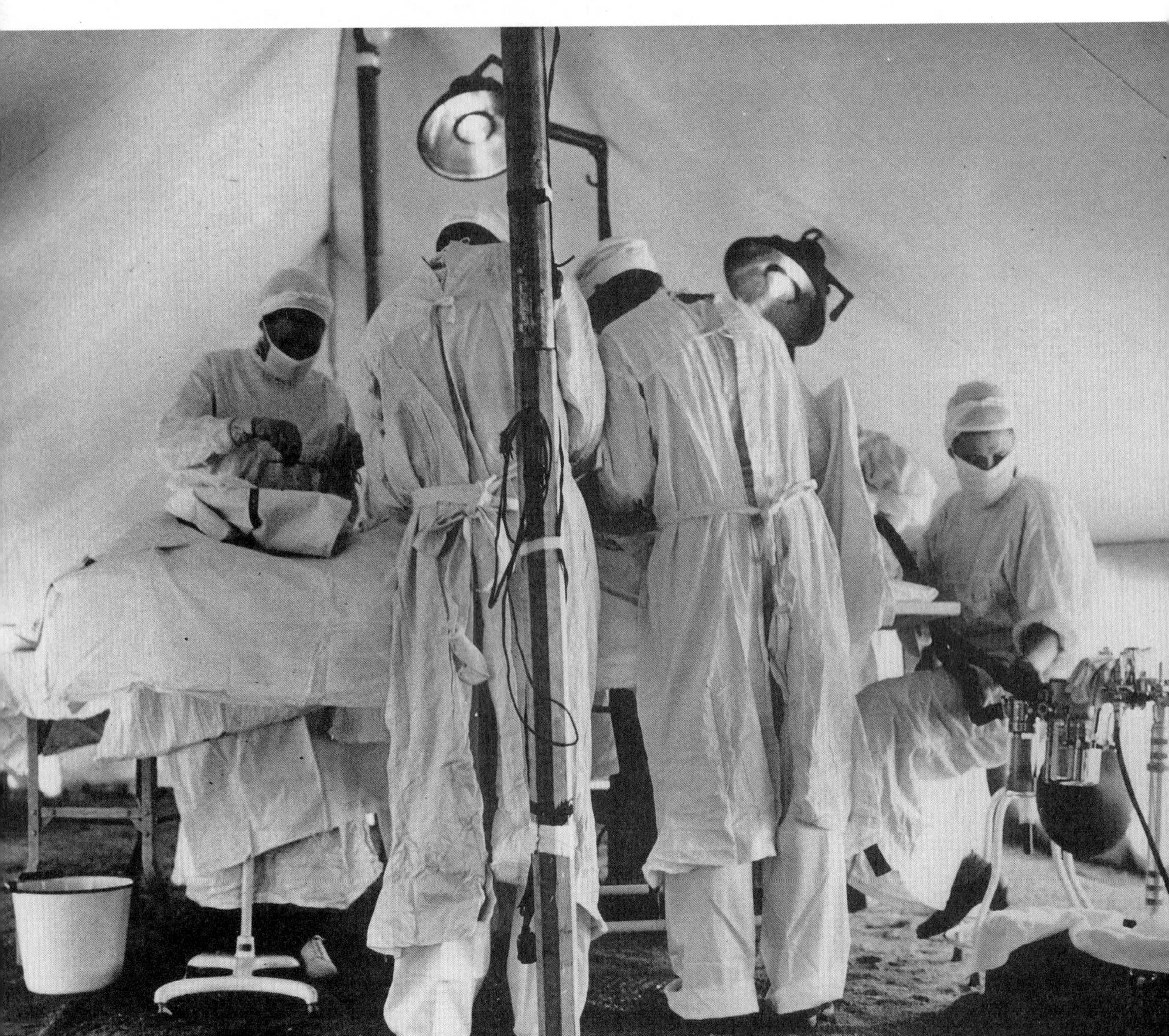

had to be stitched together or joined by a metal tube with the vessel of the person receiving the blood. The new way of transfusing blood led to the introduction of blood banks, and in 1937, Chicago's Cook County Hospital opened the first one that stored blood given by live donors.

These developments during the 1930s were among leading medical advances that improved patients' chances of surviving operations. Also during this time, surgeons developed ways that made it possible to operate safely on more parts of the body than ever before.

Conquering Shock

The conquest of shock saved many lives on and off the operating table. Shock occurs when the body loses so much blood that its circulatory system, which pumps life-giving blood throughout the body, begins to fail. By transfusing blood, doctors and surgeons could replace body fluid to fight shock.

Better Pain Control

Improved anesthesia also helped save lives. Anesthesia reduces or eliminates pain during surgery. *General* anesthesia "knocks out" the patient. *Local* anesthesia reduces or blocks pain to specific parts of the body while the patient remains awake. In 1933, doctors improved anesthesia so they could better control breathing, heart rate, and blood pressure during surgery. This also helped patients survive.

Better transfusions and anesthetics aided surgeons who worked on the lungs, intestines, and other vital organs. Before the 1930s, surgeons could do little for people with cancer of these organs. An operation was more likely to kill the patient than the disease was.

The 1930s saw several surgical "firsts" that changed this situation. For the first time, surgeons showed they could operate on the lung or the bowel with much greater effect and safety. For example, the first man to have an entire cancerous lung removed (in 1933) not only survived the operation, but was still alive 24 years later.

The many surgical breakthroughs between 1930 and 1945, plus important chemical developments such as sulfa drugs and penicillin, were especially helpful in World War II. Thousands of wounded soldiers survived because of blood transfusions and improved surgical techniques. These advances continue to save lives. ■

Battlefield surgeons operate (far left) in a tent during World War II. Blood transfusions (above) began saving many lives in the 1930s.

1939 World's Fair

"The World of Tomorrow": With this theme, the 1939 World's Fair, held in New York City, promised Americans an exciting look at the future. When President Roosevelt opened the fair, he said, "The nation's eyes are fixed on the future. Our wagon is hitched to a star . . . of progress for Mankind. . . ."

Even as the president spoke, crews from the National Broadcasting Company were putting his voice and his picture over the airwaves. The opening of the fair was the first live television news report ever broadcast. Few people, however, had TV sets to watch the event. TV was indeed still part of "the world of tomorrow."

True to its theme, the fair's many exhibits showed different visions of the future. One of the most popular was General Motors' spectacular Futurama exhibit, a model of America in 1960 designed "to demonstrate in dramatic fashion that the world, far from being finished, is hardly yet begun. . . ." An estimated 28,000 visitors a day waited in line for hours to board a "carry-go-around" that took them on a 15-minute pretend airplane trip across the United States. They saw a seven-lane cross-country highway system on which teardrop-shaped cars could travel up to 100 miles per hour. Each car's speed was controlled not by the driver but by radio control towers five miles apart, eliminating traffic accidents.

Americans living in the Futurama world of 1960, wrote *Life* magazine, "are not attached to their own homes and home towns, because trains, express highways (and, of course, planes) get them across America in 24 hours. They have the choice of all America for their two-month vacations. . . . Architecture and plane construction have been revolutionized by light, noninflammable, strong plastics from soybeans. Houses are light, graceful, and easily replaced."

To fair visitors, it all seemed like a dream. After years of economic depression and hard times, people asked whether these wonders would ever be within their reach.

World War II delayed the answer to that question. Science, medicine, and industry put their energies into winning the war. But after the war, science and technology went back to work on the world of tomorrow. And within a few years, the wonders of the 1939 World's Fair, such as TV, began to appear in homes throughout America. ■

Sculpture and architecture at the 1939 World's Fair.

Imagine that you are putting together a "world of tomorrow" show for a new world's fair. What new products would you like to see in the future? A new car that drives itself? A robot that cooks and cleans for you? Describe a product that you would like to see developed.

* This symbol before a page number indicates a photograph of the subject mentioned.

LIST OF MAPS

Credits

Photo Credits

Beaumont Enterprise: 53
The Bettmann Archives: 11a, 13, 16, 22, 24, 26, 32, 34, 36, 43ab, 48, 51, 52, 57, 60, 61ab, 66, 67, 68ab, 70, 72abc, 74, 75, 76, 79, 82b, 91
Chicago Historical Society; SDN 76,921: 55
Courtesy Cushman and Wakefield, Inc.: 80a
Courtesy Empire State Building, managed by Helmsley-Spear, Inc.: 80b
Courtesy Alan Higgens: 62
Historical Association of Southern Florida: 47ab
Library of Congress: 10, 33ab, 35, 37, 58, 84
Los Alamos National Laboratory: 86, 89a
Museum of History and Industry, Seattle, WA: 6, 38b
Museum of Modern Art/Film Stills Archive: 38a, 39ab, 41ab, 42ab, 44
Museum of the City of New York: 27
National Archives: 2a, 11b, 17, 29, 77
National Baseball Library, Cooperstown, NY: 49, 56
The National Portrait Gallery, Smithsonian Institution: 45b
The Billy Rose Theatre Collection, The New York Public Library for the Performing Arts; Astor, Lenox and Tilden Foundations: 46
Pasadena Tournament of Roses: 54
Courtesy Pictorial Parade, New York, NY: 45a
Courtesy Sylvia Zeena Ruderman Spielman, Design and Illustrations: 31
Union County Historical Society of Clayton, NM: 28
Courtesy U.S. Air Force: 3b, 89b
University Archives, University Library, University of Illinois at Chicago, Charles B. Puestow Papers: 90
Courtesy World's Fair Collectors Society, Inc.: 92

Text Credits

Interviews on pages 25–27 from *Hard Times: An Oral History of the Great Depression* by Studs Terkel. Copyright © 1970 by Studs Terkel. Reprinted by permission of Pantheon Books, a division of Random House, Inc.
Song excerpt on page 26 from "Brother, Can You Spare a Dime?" by Jay Gorney and E. Y. Harburg; © 1932 Gorney Music Publishers and Glocca Morra Music pursuant to sections 304(c) and 401(b) of the U.S. Copyright Act. All rights administered by The Songwriters Guild of America.
Song excerpt on page 29 from "Hard Travelin'." Words and music by Woody Guthrie. Copyright 1972 Ludlow Music, Inc., New York.
Novel excerpt on page 30 from *The Grapes of Wrath* by John Steinbeck. Copyright 1939, renewed © 1967 by John Steinbeck. Used by permission of Viking Penguin, a division of Penguin Books USA Inc.
Quotations on pages 34–35 reprinted by permission of The Putnam Publishing Group. Copyright © 1984 by Mark J. Harris and Steven Schechter.